Overshot Weaving

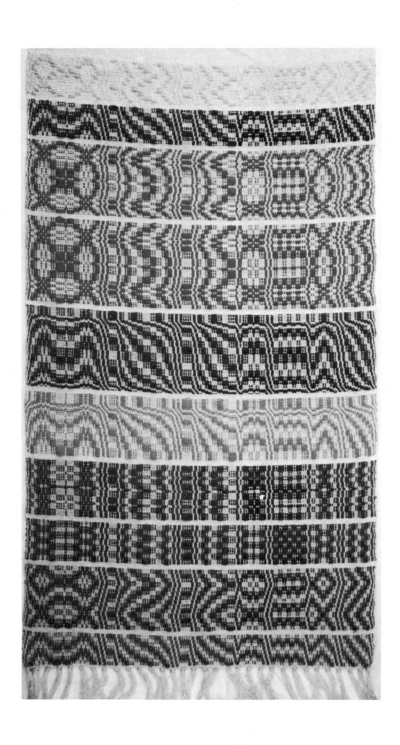

Overshot Weaving

ELLEN LEWIS SALTZMAN

 VAN NOSTRAND REINHOLD COMPANY
New York Cincinnati Toronto London Melbourne

Copyright © 1983 by Van Nostrand Reinhold Company Inc.

Library of Congress Catalog Card Number 82-13555

ISBN 0-442-21371-9

Printed in the United States of America
Designed by A. Christopher Simon

Published by Van Nostrand Reinhold Company Inc.
135 West 50th Street
New York, New York 10020

Van Nostrand Reinhold Publishers
1410 Birchmount Road
Scarborough, Ontario M1P 2E7, Canada

Van Nostrand Reinhold Australia Pty. Ltd.
480 Latrobe Street
Melbourne, Victoria 3000, Australia

Van Nostrand Reinhold Company Limited
Molly Millars Lane
Wokingham, Berkshire RG11 2PY, England

16 15 14 13 12 11 10 9 8 7 6 5 4 3 2 1

Library of Congress Cataloging in Publication Data

Saltzman, Ellen Lewis.
    Overshot weaving.

    Bibliography: p.123
    Includes index.
    1. Hand weaving. 2. Hand weaving—Patterns.
I. Title.
TT848.S25   1983   746.1   82-13555
ISBN 0-442-21371-9

To Nikki

Acknowledgments

I would like to express my deepest appreciation to the people whose work is an integral part of this book: Thomas Anderson, a good friend and talented architect, who spent hours and hours drawing the weaving diagrams; Joe Acton, who photographed the weavings with much skill and efficiency; and Irene Demchyshyn, who edited the manuscript with equal skill and many helpful ideas. Special thanks are also due to Burt, Ben and Nessa, who, without too much complaining, lived with the sound of a typewriter pounding. And thanks to all who, to me, are family and friends; all have helped in their own way.

Contents

Introduction

I had been weaving less than a year when I first encountered overshot. Having been given Marguerite Davison's *Handweaver's Pattern Book* as a gift, I tried a number of the patterns and various weave structures. One of these, Gertrude's Fancy, caught my eye. I warped the loom according to the threading draft and was hooked. Overshot began to take up more and more of my weaving time. I wove many traditional patterns and began, tentatively, to experiment with my own designs. A later opportunity to teach weaving, including overshot, helped me to learn even more. The weaving I had done previously gave me practical experience with overshot; the teaching helped me to understand theory, organize the structure, and order my practical knowledge. It also aroused my curiosity; I continued to study and weave overshot and also to learn a little bit about the history of weaving and textiles, particularly overshot and coverlet weaving, in the United States.

Without question, weaving was an essential part of domestic life in the early years of this country. Every household needed cloth for household goods such as bed linens as well as for clothing. There is, however, some disagreement as to the extent of this domestic weaving; I have read both that every house had a loom and also that this was absolutely not true. But clearly many did, and together with professional weavers, home weavers were an integral part of Colonial life. In the seventeenth and into the eighteenth centuries, weaving was primarily a domestic occupation, with some "commercialization" in the form of the small businesses of the professional weavers.

The looms used were usually quite large, made with four upright posts connected by cross beams. The harnesses, usually two or four in number, were made of strips of wood and had string heddles. These looms had overhead beaters, and a bench was usually built into the loom between the two front uprights as part of the cross beam structure. They were sizeable looms and certainly could not fit into every house, considering the space limitations of many of these dwellings. However, looms were in many households; there were, among others, large four-poster types or several kinds of smaller specialized looms, for example the lap-sized loom for weaving ribbons and tapes.

Spinning wheels, being much smaller and requiring less knowledge—although equally as much skill—to operate were more likely to be found in every household, with few exceptions. There were two main types of wheels, one being the large wheel used for spinning wool. These wool wheels (or high wheels or walking wheels) are operated by walking toward and away from the wheel as the yarn is spun. (Although yarn is measured most precisely with yards of length and pounds of weight, it is said that one could measure yarn spun on these wheels by the numbers of miles walked while spinning.) A smaller wheel used for flax spinning was known as a flax wheel, Saxony, or castle-type wheel. Unlike the wool wheel, these wheels were used sitting down.

The fibers used for spinning were flax, wool, and cotton. Flax was a widely used fiber; it could be grown relatively easily and produced a sturdy yarn. It took a full year from planting to spinning, however, to make flax into linen thread. After it was harvested, the plant had to be softened (actually rotted) to separate the usable fibers from the rest of the plant; these fibers were then processed to make them usable for spinning.

Cotton was also grown in the Colonies, primarily in the South; however, it wasn't until after the initial years of colonization that it became a fiber of great importance. In the early years, the main southern crop was tobacco, and there was little interest in producing cotton, which was harder to grow and required a great deal of processing by hand in the days before the invention of the cotton gin.

Wool was the other fiber most often used for spinning and weaving although, until sheep were raised domestically, the wool had to be imported. At first the wool was imported from England, but when this was restricted, the trade turned to Holland and Spain.

All these fibers were woven into a variety of fabrics. The earliest produced were practical in nature. In the New World fabrics were valued for their durability. There was little time or money for frivolous goods. The fabrics were woven primarily of linen or wool, in quiet colors. The weaves used were also simple and lent themselves to practical fabrics: Ms and Os, huck, honeycomb, plain, and twill weaves were among the most popular.

In general, when America was first being settled, textiles were produced through a combination of domestic production and imports. The South tended more toward imports because they had a cash crop—tobacco—to trade for imported goods. In the North and in frontier areas, home production of the essentials—such as fabrics for clothing and household uses—tended to be the rule. Again, however, there seems to be no strong evidence to support the notion that every household had a loom. In fact, there is evidence of a number of "weaving houses," where there would be enough looms for several families to use and where they could produce, or have produced, their needed fabrics. George Washington had such a weaving house at his plantation, Mount Vernon, and it apparently supplied the cloth for approximately twenty-five families.

As trade with England fluctuated, domestic production of cloth became even more important. Originally, England assumed the Colonies would be markets for England's own products and preferred not to sell raw goods to them. However, this restricting had the effect of encouraging domestic production of the raw goods. Many towns advertised for flax growers and others involved in cloth production to settle within their boundaries. When further restrictions continued to be imposed, on trade as well as on production, this fervor for domestic goods grew even larger. It was considered patriotic to produce cloth and yarn. Spinning matches were even held in order to determine which spinners were the most productive, and thus the most patriotic.

The onset of the Revolutionary War meant that all trade with England was suspended, for the duration of the war certainly, and trade with other countries was, of course, also disrupted. The Colonists had to rely on themselves for cloth and clothing. This meant great hardship, especially in the colder climates, and there was a severe lack of uniforms and warm clothing in the Continental Army. But just as war brought great deprivation, so the victorious end of the war brought exuberance, and progress, and also more wealth. Weaving became increasingly commercialized and mechanized, a process greatly aided by the invention of the power loom toward the end of the eighteenth century. The fibers and fabrics used became more decorative, with less emphasis on utility. Silks were imported for clothing and cotton became more popular as a fiber; the wools and linens of the past years, so strong and practical, became less important and desired. And home weaving was in a state of decline, beginning with the latter part of the eighteenth century and continuing into the nineteenth; it died out, with few exceptions, by the Civil War era.

The story of coverlet weaving in the United States parallels this history of weaving in general. The overshot weave came to North America with the waves of European immigrants. The earliest reliably dated overshot coverlets we have are from the middle and later eighteenth century, and appear to be from the Hudson Valley area. The exact country of origin, however, is not known; examples of weaves similar or identical to what we call overshot have been found in places ranging from Poland to Scandinavia to Greece to Wales. However, the popularity of the weave and the multitude of designs appear to have become strongest once on the North American continent.

The most widespread use of overshot was for coverlets. Blankets and bed-coverings were an essential, functional part of a household; when woven with the overshot weave, these ordinary household items became decorative as well. How wonderful it must have been to weave the needed blankets in patterns that would also brighten the house. Many homes, particularly in the North, were small, and beds were often not in separate rooms as they are today. Rather, they were in the sitting room (the other room besides the kitchen) and the importance of decorative bedcoverings is even more obvious.

Furthermore, unlike other pattern weaves, overshot weaving was within the capabilities of many home weavers with 4-harness looms. It was also standard fare for the professional weavers of the day. As a weave structure, overshot offers more pattern variety than other similar 4-harness weaves because four blocks can be formed to make the patterns. For example, with summer and winter, another popular coverlet weave, only two blocks are possible with a 4-harness loom. The Jacquard coverlets, so popular in the early nineteenth century, require a specialized loom attachment and technique and, therefore, were beyond the reach of most home weavers.

As home weaving began to die out in the late eighteenth and early nineteenth centuries, so did overshot coverlet weaving. The elaborate, often over-florid Jacquard coverlets were more popular in the period following the Revolutionary War, because this was part of the trend toward more elaborate and decorative styles in general. Clothing became more stylish, and fabrics were made of less practical fibers like silk and cotton. The Civil War, and all the disruption that it imposed, marked the end of the major era of home weaving of coverlets. Some areas of the South (mainly in Kentucky and Tennessee) continued to produce coverlets, but in New England coverlet production died out almost completely.

Handweaving has enjoyed a revival in the 1900s, but as a hobby rather than a necessity of life. Overshot was part of this revival, but only for a while. According to author-weaver Berta Frey, there was a reaction in the mid-1900s against the excessive use of the overshot weave. The emphasis moved on to textures, yarns, nature weaving—anything that was not pattern weaving and was not similar to the coverlets of by-gone days. Lately there seems to be a new interest in overshot, perhaps as part of a general inquisitiveness about our history and genealogy. Handweavers are also rediscovering the challenge of loom-controlled pattern weaves and finding them interesting to weave in addition to the so-called texture and art weaves. I once overheard two weavers who were looking at one of my overshot coverlets hanging in a craft exhibition; they said lightly as they moved quickly on, "That's nothing but pushing a shuttle back and forth from side to side." I found the comment—then and now—startling in its ignorance; all weaving could, if one wanted to, be reduced to the interlacement (with shuttle or fingers or needles) of fibers. However, there is as much planning, and designing, and skill, and technique required with pattern weaves as there is in "art" weaving.

So, for those looking to acquire these skills, this book presents classic, as-drawn-in overshot for study, beginning with the structure of the weave and ending with some of the many variations and suggestions for original overshot designing. In chapter 1, several important terms are defined; the draft notations and diagrams used in this book are also explained. Chapter 2 explores the weave structure of overshot; plain and twill weave are briefly examined as a background to the overshot weave. The basic overshot threading, the block, is defined, and the rules for using the blocks in overshot threading are stated. The focus of chapter 3 is the motifs, which are formed through the various combinations of the overshot blocks. These motifs form the basis of the multitude of overshot patterns. The threading for a sampler, consisting of all the motifs, is given here in order to allow you to practice weaving overshot and become familiar with the motifs. The motifs are in their turn combined and arranged to form patterns; a few of the many are analyzed in chapter 4. The patterns are presented with complete threading and treadling information, so they can be easily reproduced. The subjects of chapter 5 are the variations possible through alternate treadlings, and designing your own overshot patterns. With these variations, a warp threaded with overshot can produce finished pieces that are quite dissimilar; thus, different fabrics and effects can be woven with only one loom dressing. In chapter 6, twenty-five draft diagrams for overshot patterns are shown; they can be a resource for your overshot pattern weaving, or they can be used to study the various motif combinations in overshot. Both diagrams and photographs are used throughout the book to help you become familiar with both the structural basis and the woven appearance of the overshot weave.

This book is for experienced weavers who may not have experimented with overshot, but it can also be used by novices with little weaving experience. Whichever you are, I hope that studying the information presented here, and practicing the weaving as well, will be the start of your weaving with overshot.

1. Definitions

This is a book for weavers who already have some experience with looms. The basic elements of weaving and loom use—winding a warp, dressing the loom, and throwing a shuttle, for example—will not be dealt with here. It is not necessary, however, to have substantial knowledge of and experience with weave structures in order to use this book. The basic weave structures used in overshot are discussed in chapter 2. But since everyone, from beginner to expert, has his or her own set of definitions and understandings as well as individual way of weaving, defining some basic terms and the drafting conventions used throughout this book might be helpful. First, here are a few of the terms used:

block: a group of warp ends used together consistently in the threading and treadling to form a unit of the pattern structure

end: a warp thread

float: part of the pattern that occurs when weft threads pass over two or more warp ends, or when warp ends pass over two or more weft threads

shed: opening in warp through which weft passes, caused by action of harnesses rising (jack loom) or sinking (counterbalanced loom)

shed sequence: order in which harnesses or harness combinations are used to make sheds; same as treadling sequence

weaving as-drawn-in: type of weaving in which the shed sequence is identical to the threading sequence (if the warp is threaded 1,2,3,4, the harnesses will be treadled in the same order)

DRAFTS

The draft diagrams and directions in this book are written for *counterbalanced (sinking shed) looms* because, for as-drawn-in overshot, the drafts for this type of loom most clearly show the relationship between the threading structure and the woven pattern. Overshot pattern areas (floats) develop when weft threads cover groups of warp ends. These float areas are named to correspond to the harness numbers of the warp ends covered. For example, if ends in harnesses 1 and 2 are covered, that is considered a 1–2 float. With a counterbalanced loom, when harnesses 1 and 2 are treadled (lowered), those are the warp ends covered. With a *jack (rising shed) loom*, however, when harnesses 1 and 2 are treadled (raised), warp ends in harnesses 3 and 4 are covered. It is therefore easier, especially for a beginner, to visualize the woven pattern and its relationship to the threading and treadling structure when using a counterbalanced draft diagram. Converting from jack to counterbalanced and vice versa is simple, and several ways will be described below as part of the draft diagram explanation.

The *draft diagram* (fig. 1-1) is the basis of weaving notation and record keeping. It is a four-part diagram and includes the threading sequence, the tie-up, the shed sequence, and the draw-down. This information can be recorded on a draft diagram in a variety of ways; the one used here is my preference, but other styles are in use and are equally good.

Figure 1-1 shows a draft diagram as notated in this book, with the four sections marked. Section A is the *threading draft*, which gives the sequence of the warp ends as they are drawn in through the harnesses. The threading draft here is read from right to left. The vertical rows of squares represent warp ends (each row is one end), and the horizontal rows represent the harnesses. Harness 1, the one nearest the weaver sitting at the loom, is the lowest row and harness 4 the highest row. Numbers are used to indicate the harness through which each warp end will be threaded. In this example, warp end number 1 will go through a heddle on harness 1, warp end number 2 will go through a heddle on harness 2, and so on.

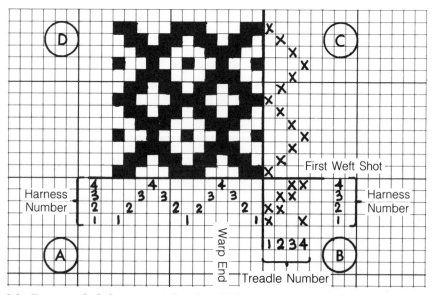

1-1. Four-part draft diagram: (A) threading draft; (B) tie-up; (C) treadling or shed sequence; (D) draw-down.

The *tie-up* is given in section *B* of the draft diagram. The tie-up indicates which harness or harnesses are connected to which treadles and used together to make the sheds. The horizontal rows here again indicate the harnesses, and the vertical rows and treadles to which the harnesses will be connected. This section is read from left to right. In this example, the first treadle is connected to harnesses 1 and 2, the second treadle to harnesses 2 and 3, the third treadle to harnesses 3 and 4, and the fourth treadle to harnesses 1 and 4. Remember, this is a tie-up for a counterbalanced loom. To convert it for a jack loom, (sinking to rising), connect the treadles to the harnesses opposite those indicated by the counterbalanced tie-up: following this diagram, the first treadle would then be connected to harnesses 3 and 4, the second treadle to harnesses 1 and 4, and so on. Figure 1-2 shows the related jack and counterbalanced tie-ups. By changing the tie-up, the pattern in figure 1-1 can be woven on a jack loom (if, on the other hand, the threading and treadling drafts in figure 1-1 were to be used on a jack loom without converting the tie-up as shown in figure 1-2, the woven pattern would not be identical, as can be seen in figure 1-3).

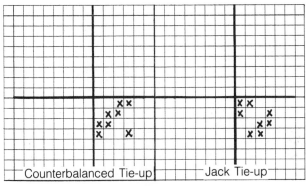

Counterbalanced Tie-up · Jack Tie-up

1.2. Converting from a counterbalanced tie-up to a jack tie-up.

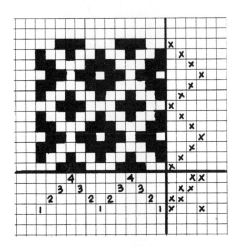

1-3. Using the identical threading, tie-up, and treadling draft diagram as in figure 1-1 will produce a different pattern on a jack (rising shed) loom.

Section C of figure 1-1 is the *treadling* (or shed sequence) *draft*. The shed sequence is the order in which the harnesses are raised or lowered to make the shed openings through which the weft is passed. Each horizontal row on the draft represents one shot of weft, and the vertical rows indicate which treadle is used for each shot. Reading from the bottom up in this section, you will see that the first shot of weft will be passed through the shed made when the first treadle is used, the second shot through the shed made when the second treadle is used, and so on, until all the shots have been thrown.

The conversion from counterbalanced to jack can be made in the treadling, or shed, sequence, if it was not done in the tie-up, by changing the shed sequence to open the correct sheds. For example, the first shed in figure 1-1 is a 1–2 shed, where all the 1–2 warp ends will be covered. With a counterbalanced loom, this shed is opened by lowering harnesses 1 and 2; with a jack loom, this shed could be opened by raising harnesses 3 and 4, and so on. Figure 1-4 shows the shed sequence that would be used to weave the same pattern as in figure 1-1, using a counterbalanced tie-up on a jack loom. This method is useful if the tie-up mechanism on your loom is difficult to change (this method of altering the shed sequence can be used in general if you don't want to change your tie-up for different patterns and weaves, not just for jack-counterbalanced conversions). The sequence can be worked out before you start to weave so that the woven pattern will be the same as the as-drawn-in one. When weaving, however, I find it more difficult to remember the treadling

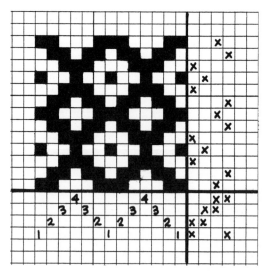

1-4. This threading and tie-up are identical to those in figure 1-1. The treadling sequence, however, is altered for a jack loom to produce the identical pattern in both drawn-downs.

sequence used in such a conversion: it does not directly reflect the threading sequence that becomes so familiar because of the time spent planning the threading draft and then threading the loom.

The *draw-down* is seen in section *D* of the draft diagram in figure 1-1. It is a representation on graph paper of the woven pattern and is arrived at by imitating the weaving process. In this section, the vertical rows represent warp ends (as in the threading section), and the horizontal rows are the shots of weft (as in the treadling section). With the tie-up given in figure 1-1 (counterbalanced), when treadle 1 is depressed, harnesses 1 and 2 will be lowered, and all the threads in those harnesses will be covered with the weft that is passed through the shed. In the draw-down, all the squares in the first horizontal row (first weft shot) that are above the ones and twos in the threading draft are filled in. Each successive row, or weft shot, is filled in this way. Draw-downs do not look exactly like a piece of weaving, but they do show the lines of the pattern on paper instead of on the loom. This is useful when trying out new patterns and when checking to see that your planned pattern has no mistakes in it. And although filling in all the squares is a time-consuming process, it is less than loom time. Using draw-downs to test patterns before weaving also has the advantage of not wasting yarns.

YARNS

The yarns used for the samples in this book were chosen to fit the overshot structure. Overshot is a compound weave, with a plain weave background and an interwoven pattern of weft floats. The plain weave is a balanced weave, and therefore the warp yarn and plain weft yarn are usually the same weight, if not actually identical. The yarn used for the weft float patterns needs to be soft enough to pack down well into the plain weave without distorting the plain weave too much. The pattern yarn should be heavier than the yarn used for the warp and plain weave weft so that the pattern will stand out strongly and will not be lost in the plain weave.

The warp and the plain weave weft yarn used in this book is a 3/12 wool worsted (approximately 2,000 yards per pound); the pattern weft yarn is a 2-ply wool (approximately 1,000 yards per pound). The warp is sleyed singly in a 12-dent reed. Traditionally, overshot was woven with lighter-weight yarns, but I have found heavier yarns to be workable. My preference is for weaving with heavier yarns, wool in particular, so I experimented with various yarns and weights until I found a successful combination. However, overshot can be woven with a variety of materials in different weights, and you should experiment with those you prefer, after becoming familiar with the weave.

2. *The Blocks*

Overshot is a compound weave: it combines a plain weave background with a weft float pattern structure. However, it is usually classified as a twill derivative weave, and in fact the pattern structure is a twill derivative independent of the plain weave background: if the floats that form the overshot pattern were to be cut away, a plain weave fabric would be left.

Overshot is also a block weave. In a block weave, groups of warp ends are used together consistently in threading and treadling to form a unit (or block) of the pattern structure. These blocks are then combined to form the patterns of overshot. There is an unending number of ways to combine the blocks, some interesting, some dull, and some simply mediocre. But, before discussing how these blocks are combined to form patterns, let us look at the structure of the blocks themselves.

PLAIN AND TWILL WEAVES

There are four basic weave structures: plain, twill, satin, and compound. These structures are, singly or in combination, the basis of all the varieties of weaves. The overshot structure involves both plain and twill weaves, as background and pattern, so a brief description of each follows.

Plain Weave

Plain weave is the alternation of warp ends and weft shots. The simplest plain weave is threaded such that the warp ends are on alternate harnesses: a 2-harness threading would be 1,2,1,2,1,2; a 4-harness threading, 1,2,3,4,1,2,3,4 (figs. 2-1 and 2-2). The threading alternation is always from odd to even or even to odd. In the draft in figures 2-1 and 2-2, the threading is in a straight sequence: from 1 to 2 or from 2 to 3, and so on. In complex weaves, such as overshot, this is not usually the case; the warp ends do not progress in a straight sequence but move back and forth, for example, 1,2,1,2,3,2,3,4,3,4. As long as the progression is from odd to even or even to odd, plain weave will result when all the odd-numbered harnesses are combined to form a shed, alternating with the shed formed by combining the even-numbered harnesses.

To weave, all the odd-numbered harnesses are treadled together for one shed opening and then all the even harnesses for the other shed opening. These sheds are commonly named *a* and *b* to indicate the alternation of the two sheds

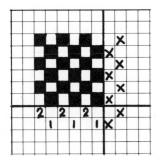

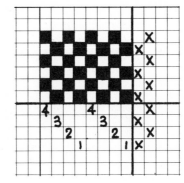

2-2. Four-harness plain weave.

2-1. Two-harness plain weave.

of plain weave. A complete draft and draw-down is shown in figures 2-1 and 2-2, giving the threading, tie-up, treadling, and draw-down for a 2-harness and a 4-harness plain weave, and a photograph of plain weave is shown in figure 2-3. The draw-downs and photograph show the balanced plain weave structure, also known as *tabby*, that is found in overshot weave. In a balanced plain weave, the warp and weft yarns are of equal weight and show equally in the finished fabric. There are also weaves that use an unequal balance between warp and weft in plain weave. This "unbalance" is achieved through varied use of yarns, setts, and beating. Tapestry, a weft-faced plain weave, is one of the best-known examples.

2-3. Four-harness plain weave.

Twill Weave

The twill structure, unlike plain weave, needs a minimum of three harnesses, though the most widely used twills involve a minimum of four harnesses. A 4-harness straight twill is threaded 1,2,3,4,1,2,3,4 (fig. 2-4). The threading must maintain the same succession from odd to even or even to odd throughout (except for broken and undulating twill, where the threading succession can be from odd to odd or from even to even in order to achieve a special effect as shown in figures 2-9 and 2-10).

To weave a balanced twill, the harnesses are combined to form sheds in what are called the *basic twill pairs*. For a 4-harness twill, the pairs are 1–2; 2–3; 3–4; and 1–4. Each harness is combined with an *adjacent* harness; thus, 2 is combined with 1 and 3, but not with 4. They are also all odd-even combinations, unlike in plain weave where all the odd and all the even harnesses are combined.

The shed sequence (or treadling order) parallels this "adjacency." Each successive harness combination treadled to produce a shed opening must have a harness in common with the preceding harness combination. For example, from 1–2 the next harness combination used can be 2–3 or 1–4, but not 3–4; from 2–3 the next harness combination can be 1–2 or 3–4, but not 1–4; and so on. This is often referred to as an *overlapping shed sequence*; each step in the shed sequence has an element in common with the preceding step. A draft and draw-down of a balanced 4-harness straight twill is given in figure 2-4 and a photograph in figure 2-5. The woven pattern develops on a diagonal line as the twill pairs are treadled in a straight, overlapping shed sequence.

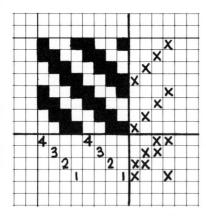

2-4. Four-harness balanced straight twill.

2-5. Four-harness balanced straight twill.

There are many variations of the basic twill threading and treadling. Figure 2-6, for example, shows a balanced point twill draft. Although the threading is more complex than for the straight twill, the basic elements are the same. The pattern develops on the diagonal, the threading progression continues odd-even, and the twill pairs form the basis of the woven pattern. Two well-known point twills are Bird's Eye and Goose Eye. Bird's Eye is simply point twill threading as shown in figure 2-6. It is a pattern of continuous twill threading, from 1 to 4 to 1 to 4, and so on. The woven pattern consists of connected diamonds, with a small dot in the center of each. In Goose Eye (fig. 2-7), there are separate point twills going in opposite directions. The threading progresses from 1 to 4 to 1, then 4 to 1 to 4, in alternation. The pattern reflects this threading and has separated diamonds, also with a small dot in the center of each. Goose Eye is often threaded with straight twill lines between the point twills, and this has the effect of separating the diamonds even more.

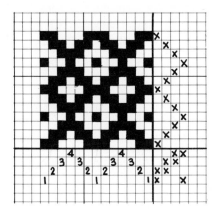

2-6. Four-harness balanced point twill (also known as Bird's Eye).

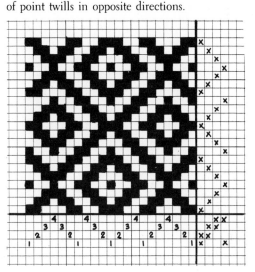

2-7. Goose Eye point twill. The pattern consists of point twills in opposite directions.

Other twill variations might involve altering the sheds or modifying the odd-even progression in the threading. Figure 2-8 shows an *unbalanced* twill, which results from not using the basic twill pairs for the harness combinations. The threading and treadling sequence is the same as for figure 2-4, but the harness combinations have been changed so that each shed is made up of three harnesses. The twill line is thicker than it is when woven with two harnesses in combination.

2-8. Four-harness unbalanced straight twill. Note the thicker pattern line.

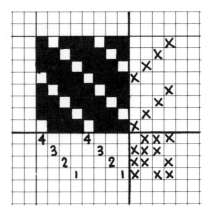

In other variations, the odd-even progression in the threading is altered; broken and undulating twills are examples of this. The draft diagram of a broken twill is shown in figure 2-9; in this type of twill a warp end is eliminated just before or after the point. This shrinks the weft float at the point to only two ends (compare this to the three-end float at the point in figure 2-6). This shorter float results in a stronger and tighter fabric. In undulating twills (fig. 2-10), warp ends are added to elongate some parts of the twill line, giving a wavy, fluid look to the pattern line. In both the broken and undulating twills, the odd-even progression is interrupted.

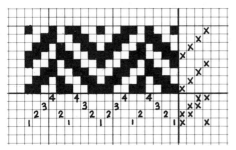

2-9. Four-harness broken twill. A warp end has been eliminated just after the first point and just before the last point.

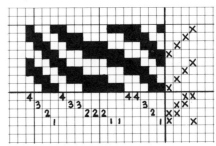

2-10. Four-harness undulating twill. Note the repeating warp ends and the wavy twill line.

OVERSHOT

Overshot combines a plain weave background with an interwoven pattern of weft floats; the pattern structure of the weft floats is based on the twill pairs. The pattern and background can be seen when examining a piece of overshot fabric (fig. 2-11). It is a three-part fabric, consisting of a balanced plain weave (tabby) background (A), pattern areas of weft floats (B), and areas of a mixture of the two, called half-tones (C). (By comparing figs. 2-11 and 2-12, you will see that overshot is not a reversible weave. The front and back are *not* identical patterns in positive and negative: if plain weave is seen on one side, weft floats are on the other side, and vice versa; the half-tones, however, are the same on both sides.) Overshot is also a three-thread construction, consisting of the warp ends, the background (tabby) weft, and the pattern weft. In the actual weaving process, the warp and tabby weft yarns are usually the same; the pattern weft yarn is of a heavier-weight yarn.

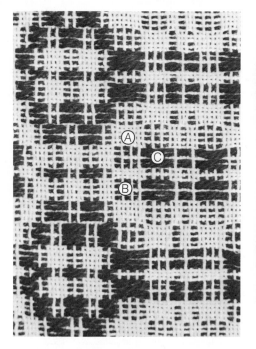

2-11. Top side of overshot fabric, showing the three parts of the weave: (A) plain weave background; (B) weft floats; (C) half-tones.

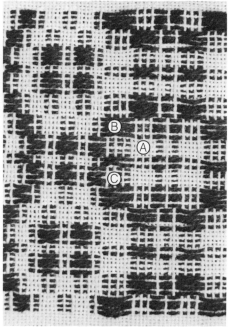

2-12. Reverse side of fabric shown in 2-11. The reverse side does not have an identical pattern: the reverse of the weft floats is plain weave and vice versa; the half-tones are found in the same area on both sides.

Overshot uses the basic twill pairs (1–2; 2–3; 3–4; and 1–4) and expands them into *blocks*. To thread the overshot blocks, these pairs are expanded to a minimum of four ends. The blocks are most commonly lettered to name them: the basic 4-harness overshot blocks are threaded A = 1,2,1,2; B = 2,3,2,3; C = 3,4,3,4; and D = 4,1,4,1. As with the twill pairs, the blocks are built with odd-even, adjacent combinations. This adjacency is again evident when the blocks are combined into overshot threadings. The threading progression must be from one adjacent block to another; each successive block must have a thread in common with the previous block (like the overlapping shed sequence of the twill weave). Thus, from A the threading may proceed to B or D (from 1,2 to 2,3 or 4,1) but not C (3,4); from B to C or A, but not D; from C to D or B, but not A; and from D to A or C, but not B.

Figure 2-13 shows a simple overshot *threading draft* of a *straight progression* of blocks, with four ends in each block (in a straight progression, the sequence follows an alphabetical or numeric order—such as 1,2,3,4 and A,B,C,D— rather than skipping around—such as 1,3,4,2). In overshot, blocks threaded in a straight progression always have an even number of ends. Notice that, in the threading of adjacent blocks, the last warp end in each block is the same as the first warp end of the next block. *This end is eliminated in actual use:* the first warp end of any block will be the last warp end of the previous block, and vice versa. The actual threading draft is shown in figure 2-14. The arrows indicate the common ends between the adjacent blocks.

2-13. Straight-progression threading of overshot blocks.

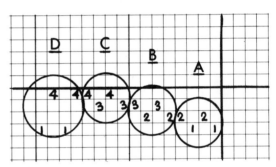

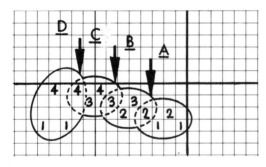

2-14. Actual threading draft of straight progression of blocks, with common threads between blocks indicated by arrows and blocks indicated by letters.

The tie-up (or harness combinations) used to weave traditional, as-drawn-in overshot is based on the twill pair combinations and the related overshot blocks. The harnesses are combined 1–2; 2–3; 3–4; and 1–4 to form the sheds for weaving the pattern and the half-tones. Two plain weave sheds are also needed to weave the background—1–3 and 2–4. Using these combinations, the harnesses corresponding to the order of the blocks are treadled; for example, to weave pattern block A, the 1–2 shed is opened. The sheds are opened in the same order that the blocks are threaded.

The *number of shots* of pattern weft per block is determined by the number of warp ends in that block: it is one less than the number of threads contained in the block. This takes into account the common thread between the blocks. I call it the *One-less Rule*. Since blocks in a straight progression have an *even* number of threads, they will always have an *odd* number of shots of pattern weft. A shot of tabby is thrown in between each pattern shot, with the tabby alternating a,b,a,b. The sequence for an A block with four threads is 1–2,a,1–2,b,1–2,a; for B it is 2–3,a,2–3,b,2–3,a; and so on. This is shown in figure 2-15, with a complete draft and draw-down.

Including both the pattern shots and the tabby in the draw-down, however, is quite cumbersome to continue throughout an entire overshot draft and tends to mask the block pattern. The tabby sequence, therefore, is usually eliminated on the draft, and only the draw-down of the blocks is seen. *In actual practice, the tabby is always woven.* Figure 2-16 shows the abbreviated draw-down for the draft in figure 2-15. The tabby shots have been eliminated; each block is woven for three shots.

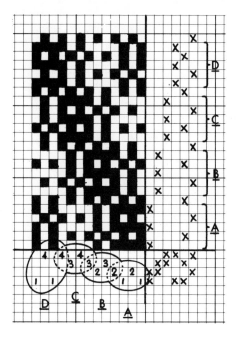

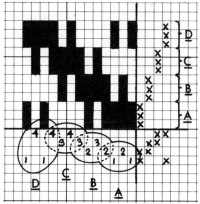

2-15. Draft diagram of overshot blocks in straight progression. This example includes a draw-down of tabby shots between each pattern shot.

2-16. Draft diagram of overshot blocks in straight progression, with tabby shots eliminated in draw-down.

A smaller area of weft can be seen on each side of the blocks. These are the *half-tones*, indicated by arrows in figure 2-17. Half-tones are pattern areas where individual warp ends, rather than groups of warp ends, are covered by the pattern weft. Half-tones are formed by the common warp ends in the adjacent blocks in the following way. Blocks are threaded such that they are adjacent; each block has a common end with the preceding one. For example, block A is threaded 1,2,1,2, and block B is threaded 2,3,2,3 (remember, in actual practice the last 2 in A and the first 2 in B are the same warp end). When the 1–2 shed is opened and a pattern shot thrown to weave block A, all warp ends in harnesses 1 and 2 will be covered by the pattern weft. These ends include all the ones and twos in block A as well as the ones and twos in blocks B (2,3,2,3) and D (4,1,4,1). These warp ends in B and D work

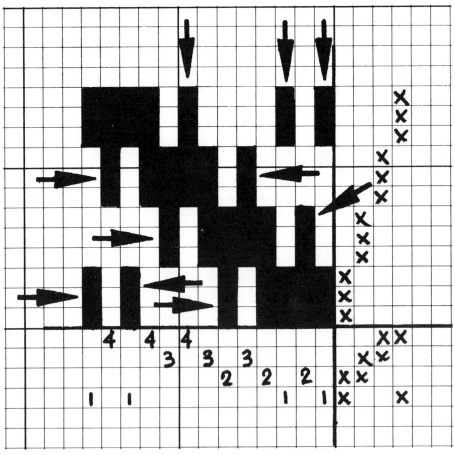

2-17. Overshot blocks. The half-tones are indicated by arrows.

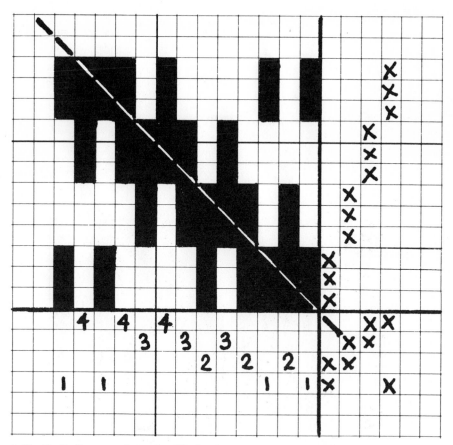

2-18. Draft diagram of overshot blocks showing 45° diagonal that develops from the lower right-hand corner of each block.

individually, not as part of a block or unit, and they are covered by the weft individually—and so the half-tones are produced. The number of half-tones surrounding a pattern area is determined by the size of the adjacent blocks. The more ends that there are in the adjacent block, the larger the area of half-tones will be.

The overshot *pattern*, when woven as-drawn-in, develops on the diagonal, as is the case with the twill pattern. Each successive pattern block area overlaps the previous block by one warp end (the common end) and then covers as many warp ends as are in the block. A 45° diagonal develops from the beginning corner of the first block and the beginning corner of each successive pattern area (fig. 2-18).

Overshot patterns would be quite tedious if all they did was develop in a straight line. Most patterns include straight lines as well as turning points and reversals, similar to the ones found in twill variations previously discussed. Figure 2-19 shows an overshot pattern with a return, like the point twill. Note that at the turning block (D in this instance), there is an *uneven* number of warp ends; this is true of all turning blocks. This uneven number allows the threading to continue in an odd-even progression, and it maintains the symmetry of the pattern since the blocks mirrored on either side of the turning block will be of the same size. In a pattern drafted A,B,C,D,C,B,A the symmetry is preserved if both A blocks and both B blocks and both C blocks have the same number of warp ends on either side of the central D block.

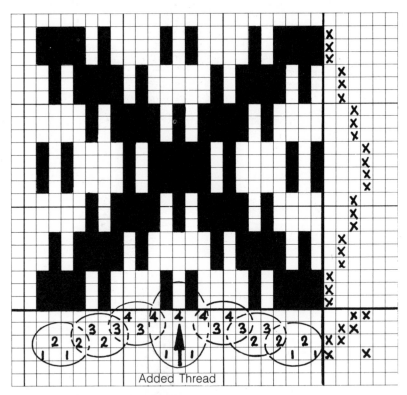

2-19. Draft diagram of overshot blocks in return pattern. A thread has been added to the center turning block (D).

A warp end can be added (as in fig. 2-19) or subtracted (as in fig. 2-20) from the block, depending on the motif in which that block is contained and the number of threads in the block. Since the number of pattern shots in weaving an overshot block is one less than the number of threads in the block, turning blocks will always be woven with an even number of shots.

Although making the pattern symmetrical around the center is now accepted practice, this was not always the case. Symmetry was the rule in coverlets produced in New England, but not in the ones woven in the southern United States. As Mary Meigs Atwater so crisply notes in *The Shuttle-craft Book of American Handweaving*, "The New England weavers did not tolerate such lopsidedness, and it does not appear to be a thing worth preserving." An examination of the Canadian coverlets and drafts in *Keep Me Warm One Night*, by Harold and Dorothy Burnham, shows many coverlets with uneven blocks,

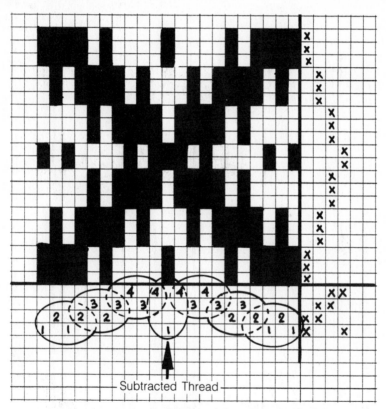

2-20. Same as figure 2-19, but with thread subtracted from the turning block instead of added to it.

or lines where the odd-even threading sequence was not maintained. The Burnhams, however, do not agree with Atwater; they feel that the symmetrical rearrangement of traditional patterns does not necessarily enhance the pattern and "the results often die of perfection." History aside, I recommend using an uneven number of threads in the turning block.

This description of how to thread, treadle, and weave basic as-drawn-in overshot has in it elements that will carry over to its drafting and weaving (such as the structure of the blocks), but some elements will vary in the actual weaving process. For example, if the threading, sett, yarn balance, and beat are all in perfect relationship to each other, achieving the squared weaving that is possible on graph paper, then the number of shots for each pattern block follows the One-less Rule. In actuality, this is often not the case, whether accidentally—through choice of yarns or the wrong beat—or deliberately—to obtain a specific effect (some patterns are very attractive elongated instead of squared). The number of pattern shots per block will, therefore, stray from the theoretical, both in number and in odd versus even.

SUMMARY

Overshot is a compound block weave, with a pattern of weft floats in a twill derivative structure, on a plain weave foundation. It is a three-thread weave: warp, pattern weft, and tabby weft. There are four blocks in 4-harness overshot: A = 1,2,1,2; B = 2,3,2,3; C = 3,4,3,4; and D = 4,1,4,1. These blocks are threaded progressively and adjacently to form overshot patterns: each successive block must have an even number of warp ends and turning blocks an odd number of warp ends.

To weave, sheds are opened paralleling the block structure: 1–2; 2–3; 3–4; 1–4. There are also two tabby sheds: 1–3; 2–4. The blocks are woven by using the matching shed, the number of pattern shots being one less than the number of warp ends in that block. A shot of tabby is thrown between each pattern shot.

3. The Motifs

The basic unit of the overshot weave structure is the block; this consists of groups of warp ends used together as a unit of pattern structure. The basic units of traditional overshot patterns are *motifs*, which are combinations of the blocks in a particular format or order. The motifs are then, in turn, combined to form patterns, which are varied arrangements of motifs. There are a few basic motifs and many variations on these, from which a multitude of patterns can be made. A thorough understanding of these motifs will give you greater freedom in designing your own overshot patterns as well as greater skill in reproducing traditional ones.

The basic motifs discussed here are cross/diamond, table, star, radiating, and wheel. (Keep in mind that the appearance of a motif does not always reflect its traditional, colorful name.) Also included here are the straight line and twill-and-overshot combinations. While these are not true motifs, they are important components of many patterns and are useful tools for designing overshot. A complete draft and draw-down, and a photograph, are presented with each motif. Tabby is eliminated in the drafts, but, once again, keep in mind that it must always be woven.

And, finally, a plan for an overshot sampler will be given. This sampler includes the threading and treadling for the basic overshot motifs described here. It is a project designed to provide practice in weaving overshot, especially for those with limited experience with two-shuttle weaves. Weaving the sampler will also provide hands-on experience in applying your new overshot knowledge, helping you to become familiar with the interactions of the motifs.

CROSS/DIAMOND

This motif is one whose appearance clearly reflects its name (figs. 3-1 and 3-2). It is one of the most common figures in overshot patterns, and there are few patterns without some form of the cross or diamond in them. The *cross* is a straight progression of blocks, with a reversal at the central block back to the beginning.

The threading draft in figure 3-1 starts with block A, but using this block

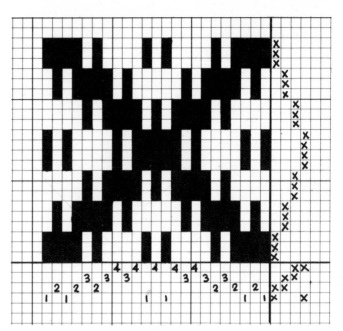

3-1. Cross motif. This is a straight progression of blocks
with a reversal at the center block.

to start the motif is an arbitrary decision. The patterns and motifs can start on
varying blocks: *it is not the starting block that is important, but rather the
order, or format, of the blocks.* The same cross will result if the draft starts on
another block, but the order (a straight progression with a reversal on the center
block) must remain the same. Figure 3-3 gives a draft diagram of a cross
beginning with block C; clearly the drawn-down pattern is identical in appearance to the cross in figure 3-1. This is important to understand, since
many identical or similar overshot patterns are drafted with different blocks and
with different starting points. You cannot rely on the named blocks to identify
a pattern or motif; you must examine the *order* of the blocks. The starting
blocks of the other motifs in this chapter will be varied to emphasize this point.

The *diamond* (figs. 3-4 and 3-5) is woven using the cross threading, but the
treadling, or shed sequence, is different. It starts with the center block rather
than with the first one. This is seen in figures 3-4 and 3-5, a four-block
diamond. Like the cross, the threading in this draft progresses straight through
four blocks from A to D, reverses on D, and returns to A. However, the
treadling starts with the 1–4 shed (D, or middle, block) and not the 1–2 shed
(A, or first, block): the threading is A,B,C,D,C,B,A and the shedding sequence
is D,C,B,A,B,C,D. The number of shots does not change, still determined

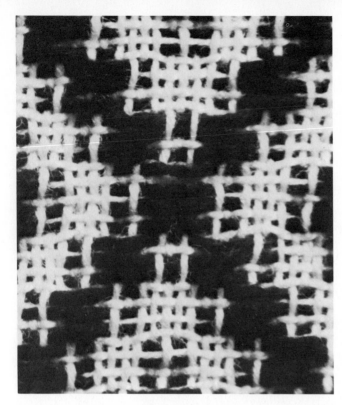

3-2. Cross motif.

3-3. Cross motif, using different blocks, but with same pattern resulting as in figure 3-1. Since both are as-drawn-in, the treadling sequence changes to reflect the change in threading order.

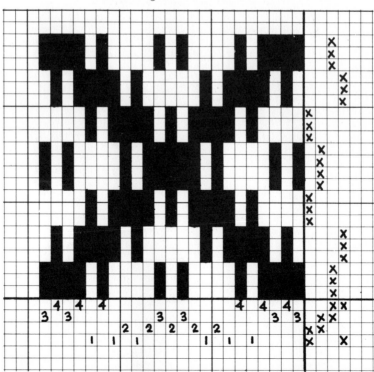

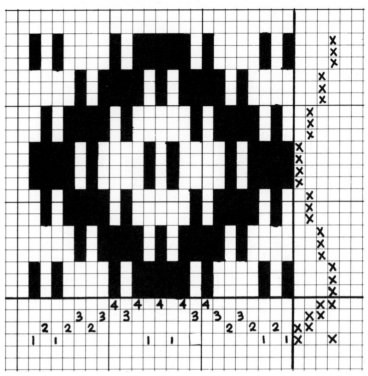

3-4. Four-block diamond motif. The diamond has the same threading as the cross, but the treadling starts with the middle (in this case *D*) block.

3-5. Four-block diamond motif.

by the One-less Rule. All blocks except the center turning block have an even number of threads and an odd number of shots; the turning block, which has an added warp end, has an odd number of threads and an even number of shots.

Other diamond motifs can be more complex and can contain more blocks. Figure 3-6 gives the draft and draw-down, and figure 3-7 a photograph of a five-block diamond. There is a straight progression here through five blocks before reversing and returning to the starting block (A,B,C,D,A,D,C,B,A). A weft float pattern appears in the center of a five-block diamond (compare this to the half-tones seen in the four-block diamond in figure 3-5). With a six-block diamond (figs. 3-8 and 3-9), there is an even larger pattern area in the center.

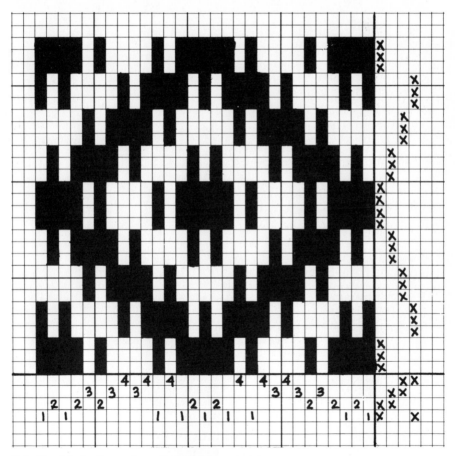

3-6. Five-block diamond motif. This has a straight progression through five blocks before reversing.

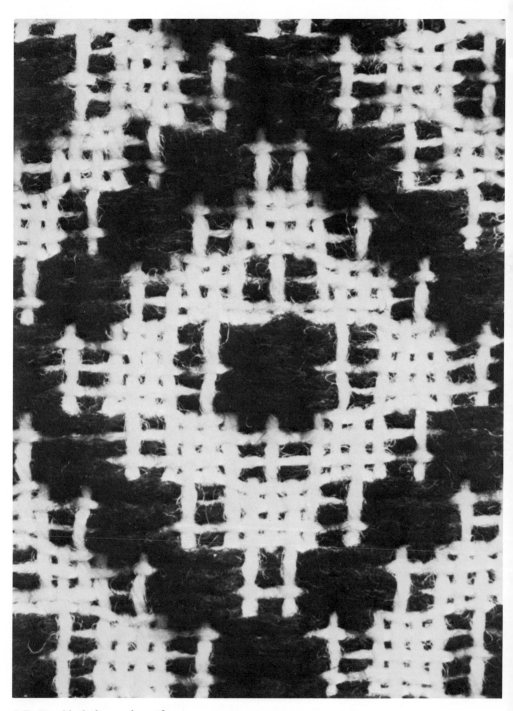

3-7. Five-block diamond motif.

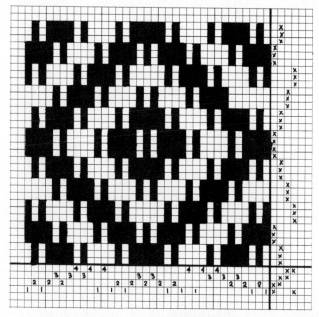

3-8. Six-block diamond motif. This has a straight progression through six blocks before reversing.

3-9. Six-block diamond.

TABLE

The table is an alternation of two blocks, with a minimum of seven repeats (figs. 3-10 and 3-11). The effect is that of a solid, square area, much like a table top, and this motif is used to separate other pattern areas or in combination with more intricate motifs (see fig. 4-15, the Double Bow Knot pattern, where the solid table area provides some "quiet" in contrast to the radiating lines of the leaf motif). The draft and draw-down of a table on blocks B and C is given in figure 3-10 and a photograph in figure 3-11. Each block in a table is a turning block since the blocks are always reversing. Thus, each block has an uneven number of warp ends and an even number of weft shots for weaving.

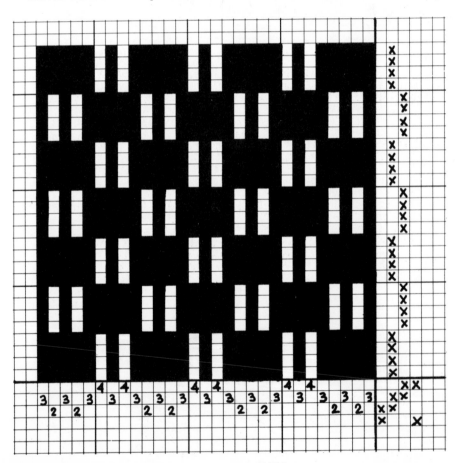

3-10. Table motif. This motif has an alternation of blocks
B and C, where B and C have the same number of threads
per block.

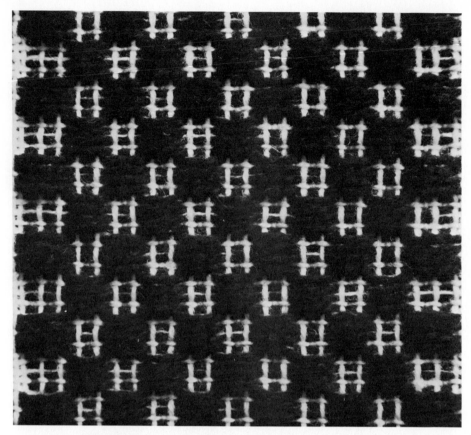

3-11. Basic table motif.

In this type of table, the blocks all have the same number of threads. There are variations, known as "fancy" tables, where the blocks are not all the same size. One variation has an uneven, but consistent, repetition of the block size, as shown in figures 3-12 and 3-13: block B consistently has three warp ends, and block C seven warp ends, across the table. Another variation is shown in figures 3-14 and 3-15, where the blocks are *not* of consistent size throughout the motif. Block B has three warp ends in one place and seven in another; C has seven in some places, five in others, and three in still others. This second variation is more intricate in appearance than the first one and breaks up the solid area more. However, the overall effect of a solid, square area is the same in both variations.

The first and last B blocks in figure 3-14 have four ends, in contrast to the odd-numbered B blocks in the rest of the table. This happens when motifs are combined into patterns, and the starting or ending block of the motif is in a straight progression with blocks around it. For example, the table in figure 3-14 is threaded B,C,B,C . . . C,B. If the block immediately preceding or following the table is an A block, then there is a straight progression from A to B, and B will have an even number of ends (picking up a common thread from the A block).

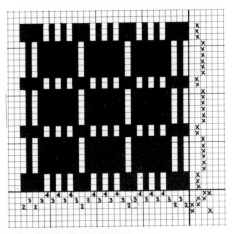

3-12. "Fancy" table with uneven but consistent number of threads per block. Block B always has three threads, and C always has seven.

3-13. "Fancy" table.

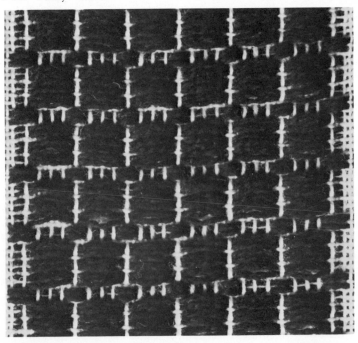

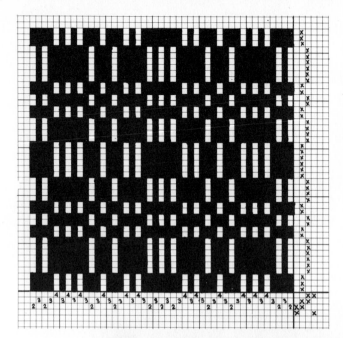

3-14. "Fancy" table with inconsistent block size. Block B has three threads in one place and five in others; block C has seven, five, or three.

3-15. "Fancy" table.

STAR

A star motif is also formed by alternating two blocks; but it usually has five sections, and the center section is smaller than the two outside blocks. Although one can imagine that the outer blocks are the points of a star, this is one motif that only somewhat resembles its name. A draft and draw-down for a basic star motif on blocks C and D is shown in figure 3-16 and a photograph in figure 3-17.

3-16. Basic star motif. This motif has an alternation of two blocks, usually with five sections.

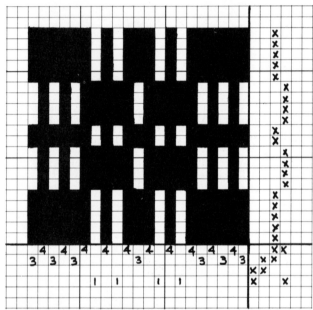

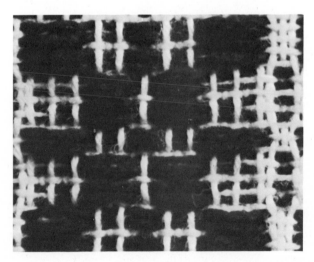

3-17. Star motif.

The basic star motif may be varied, or "fancified," like the table. One method might be to vary the number of sections in the central part of the star (figs. 3-18 and 3-19). Here the central block C of the basic star (fig. 3-16) is replaced by a C,D,C set of blocks, with the minimum number of ends in each. It is a heavier, more complex figure than the basic motif, but this configuration sets off the corner blocks (or "points"), emphasizing the starlike quality of the motif.

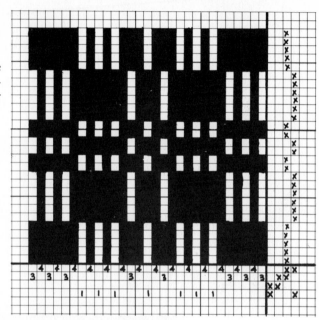

3-18. "Fancy" star. The center turning block is replaced by three smaller blocks.

3-19. "Fancy" star.

Another "fancy" star involves altering the size relationships of the blocks: the outer blocks are made smaller and the inner blocks larger (figs. 3-20 and 3-21). This variation changes the appearance of the star configuration substantially, making it less starlike and somewhat roundish.

The best-known variation of the star is a treadling variation that changes the star figure to a *rose* figure. In a treadling variation the threading is unchanged; the change is in the shed sequence, the order in which harness combinations are treadled. (One type of treadling variation was described in the cross/diamond section: by changing the order of the treadling sequence, a diamond pattern can be woven instead of a cross, with the same threading used for both motifs.) The treadling variation that converts star motifs into rose motifs is a major one, however, and it will be discussed in the section on alternate treadlings, in chapter 5.

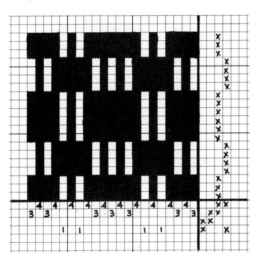

3-20. "Fancy" star. The outer blocks are smaller and the center block larger than in regular star.

3-21. "Fancy" star.

RADIATING MOTIFS

In a radiating-type motif, the blocks are drafted in repeats of a straight progression, but as the progression is repeated the blocks change size. There are two main radiating motifs: sunrise and leaf. In the *sunrise*, blocks increase in size as they move away from the center (figs. 3-22 and 3-23). In the *leaf* variety, the size of the blocks increases and then decreases as they move away from the center (figs. 3-24 and 3-25). The leaf name is particularly descriptive and the woven pattern remarkably reminiscent of the pointed ovals of many leaves. The sunrise motif is less pictorial, although one can easily imagine the swelling lines from the large, central block as the rays of the sun. Only one repeat of each motif is shown in the diagrams and photographs; however, these motifs are most often threaded with a mirror image.

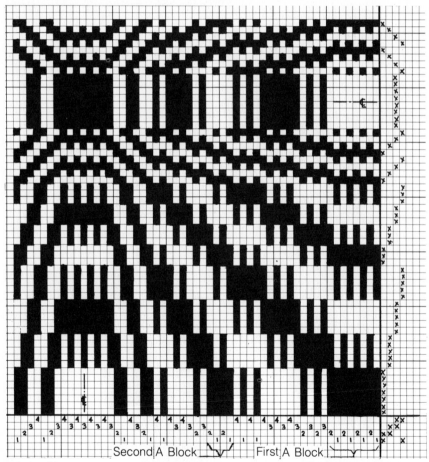

3-22. Radiating sunrise motif. The blocks increase in size as they move away from large center block. The center line of the motif (end of one repeat, reversal point) is indicated, and the start of the mirror image threading is also shown.

In both motifs, the blocks are woven square, according to the One-less Rule. The pattern line that runs down the center of the motif is straight and square; the radiating effect is achieved with the lines around the central straight line. For example, in figure 3-22 the first block (A) is threaded with eight ends in it and is woven for seven shots. The second time that the A block appears, it has only four ends in it but is also woven for seven shots; this second A block looks tall, not square, as does the entire line that develops upward from it. Conversely, when this second A block is woven in its turn with the appropriate three shots, the first A block with eight ends in it appears flat and unsquare, and the line that develops from this block appears horizontally elongated. The leaf pattern develops with a similar pattern, except that the blocks increase and decrease in size, so that the unsquare lines are elongated both horizontally and vertically.

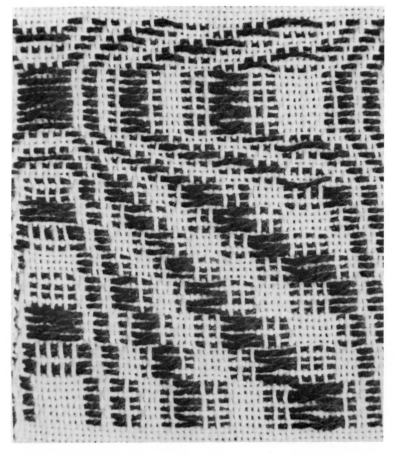

3-23. Sunrise motif.

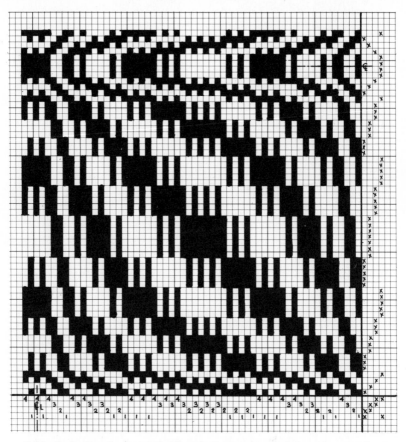

3-24. Radiating (leaf) motif. The blocks increase and then decrease in size as they move away from center block. Center line and beginning of reverse also indicated here.

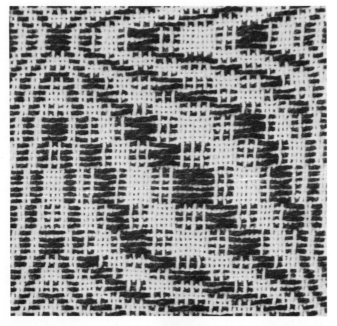

3-25. Leaf motif.

Radiating motifs are very strong patterns visually, and careful thought must go into the way in which they are combined with other motifs. They are frequently combined with tables or other solid areas of pattern (see figs. 4-13 and 4-15).

WHEEL

The wheel is a circular figure, as the name suggests; it is formed through the use of elongated lines, similar to the radiating motifs. It is not a simple circle made with one curved line: the circle is formed with elongated and foreshortened lines of overshot blocks. Picture a straight, diagonal line; if this line is elongated horizontally at the bottom and vertically at the top, a curve is the result (fig. 3-26). This is basically how the curved line is formed in overshot—by taking the straight line and elongating it in the right places. This could be achieved by increasing or decreasing the size of the blocks through varying the number of ends and/or shots in the appropriate places. The draft and draw-down in figure 3-27 demonstrates the effects that varying the size of the blocks and the number of shots can have. At the beginning of the threading draft, the blocks

3-26. Horizontal and vertical elongation of straight line to achieve curve.

3-27. The effects of varying the size of the blocks and the number of shots.

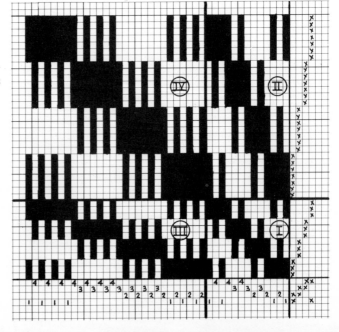

have four ends. The size increases to blocks of eight ends as the threading draft progresses. The threading draft is treadled and drawn-down as-drawn-in. In the lower right-hand section (*I*), the blocks are treadled with the correct number of shots required by the One-less Rule, and a straight line develops. In section *II*, the same threading is treadled with more shots than are called for in the One-less Rule; these blocks are not square and are too tall, giving the appearance of a vertically elongated line. When the number of shots used in weaving is fewer than the One-less Rule calls for, in relation to the size of the block, the blocks will be unsquare but too short; thus the line appears to be elongated horizontally, as in section *III*. In section *IV*, the number of shots used to weave each block corresponds to the One-less Rule, and the line develops straight and square; however, the line is thicker and larger than in section *I*, since each block contains more ends.

Using an increasing number of threads per block to achieve curved lines and circles is not always practical in overshot drafting. The number of ends in the block determines the size of the weft float, and for practical purposes this must be limited. If the float is too long, the yarn will catch and snag easily and will wear out more quickly. The float area will also have a stringy look. The usual limit is less than an inch per float, or even better, 3/4 of an inch. The elongation necessary for the wheel motif is therefore accomplished by pausing in the progression and drafting two-block alternations in appropriate places; this is shown in figure 3-28. The lowest part of the curve is drafted on blocks B and C. There are seven repeats of the two blocks, for a total of twenty-seven ends. If only one block is used to achieve this horizontal elongation, using a warp

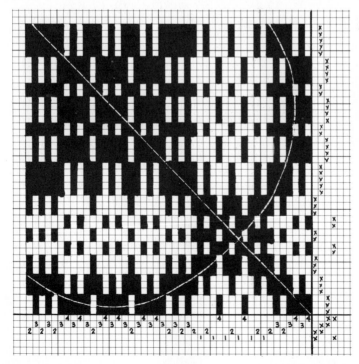

3-28. Elongation of straight line of overshot blocks by "pausing" in the progression, and drafting two-block alternation.

set at twelve ends per inch, this creates a float that is more than two inches long! This B–C alternation is also found at the beginning of the threading draft and forms the side of the circle when it is woven. Blocks A and D alternate between the two B–C sections, forming the connection between the other arcs of the circle. The 45° diagonal has been maintained, but a circular figure is achieved. To make the complete wheel, the block sequence is drafted along with its mirror image, as in figure 3-29. A photograph of this wheel draft is seen in figure 3-30.

Wheel motifs are difficult to design and to weave; the balance between warp and weft as well as the proportion between the pauses (alternation sections) of the draft are easily lost. Figure 3-31 shows a wheel with pauses not in proper proportion. There is too large an alternation in the outer A–B sections and too small an alternation in the central A–B star. The figure is diamondlike rather than circular when woven square. Because a drafted circle often turns

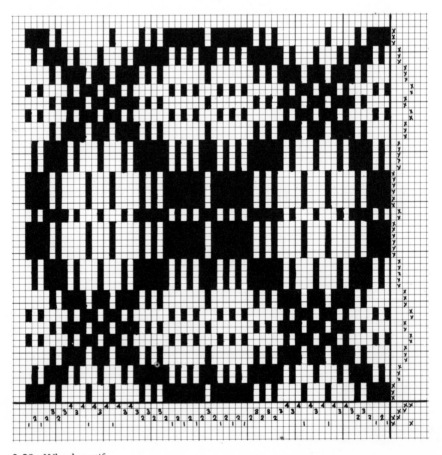

3-29. Wheel motif.

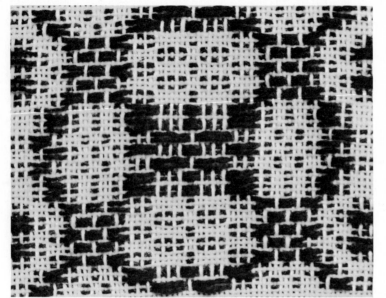

3-30. Wheel motif.

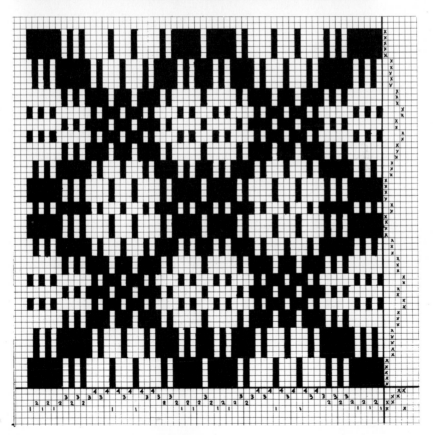

3-31. Incorrect wheel motif. The pauses are not in proper proportion, resulting in an oval figure.

out to be an oval when woven, this motif requires careful drafting. This is one
motif I keep extra precise records of, including warp, weft, draft, sett, beat,
and number of shots. Once I have discovered a successful combination, I do
not want to lose it!

STRAIGHT LINE

Although the straight line is not usually included in a discussion of overshot
motifs, I find the line a useful concept to include here. The draft for a line
is simple; it is a straight progression of blocks, as described in chapter 2. The
draft for a straight line is given in figure 3-32 and a photograph in figure 3-33.
The length of the line is determined by the number of blocks that are threaded
and treadled in straight progression.

The line is used to separate parts of patterns when this is desirable. How
long the line is will affect the look of the pattern, making it larger or smaller
and its parts more or less discrete. For example, figure 3-34 shows a simple
pattern consisting of star motifs separated by straight lines. In this draft there
is one line of straight blocks, and the star motifs are close together and look
connected. In figure 3-35, the same star motifs are separated by two lines of
straight blocks, and the stars are very separate.

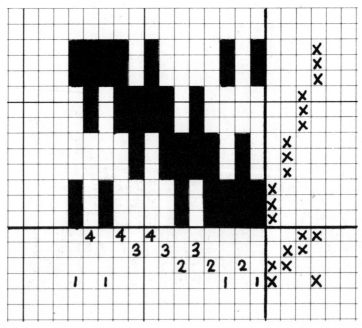

3-32. Straight line. This shows a straight progression of overshot blocks.

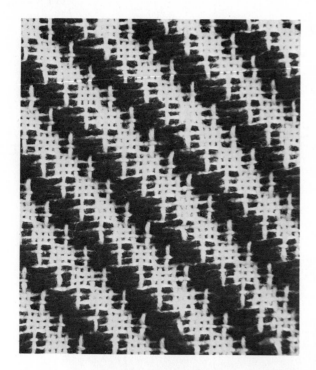

3-33. Straight line.

3-34. Star motifs separated by one straight line of blocks.

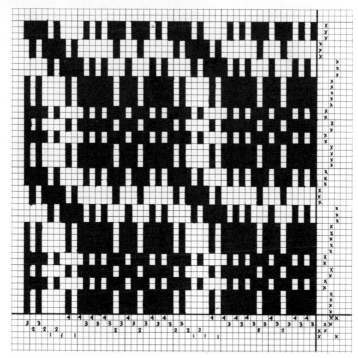

3-35. Star motifs separated by two lines, giving a more separate look to the motifs.

TWILL AND OVERSHOT COMBINATIONS

The use of twill with overshot is not strictly a motif either, but it is a very common pattern element, so it is also included here. In this type of pattern, twill threadings are mixed in with the overshot block threading. The twill lines are woven as twill in that there is only one weft shot for each twill pair; but they are also woven as overshot because a shot of tabby is thrown between each pattern shot, including the twill.

This mixture of twill and overshot is commonly found in two places. One is the radiating-type patterns, where the use of the twill threading heightens the radiating effect (see fig. 3-22). Using the twill lines allows the radiating lines to go from very narrow to much wider (twill lines to overshot lines). If these patterns were to be drafted using only the overshot blocks, they would start with blocks of four ends (the minimum number of ends) and thus would have very little distance to travel before the block size became too impractical.

The other type of pattern that uses twill frequently is the class of patterns called *miniatures*. This is a very descriptive name, and in fact these twill-overshot patterns tend to be much smaller than other overshot patterns. The miniatures use small blocks and also use twill threadings extensively with the overshot blocks. The pattern looks small when woven and has a small number of ends in the total pattern repeat.

An example of a miniature pattern is given in figure 3-36, with a photograph in figure 3-37. This threading is based on the Goose Eye twill, which has two point twill threadings in opposite directions. The first point here is an expanded point twill with several overshot blocks. It is threaded A,B,C,B,C,B,A; the central C,B,C blocks have been expanded into overshot blocks, while the side sections are twill lines. The opposite point twill in the second part of the pattern is threaded D,C,B,A,B,C,D; here only the central A block has been expanded into an overshot block. This threading (with the overshot blocks circled) is shown in figure 3-38.

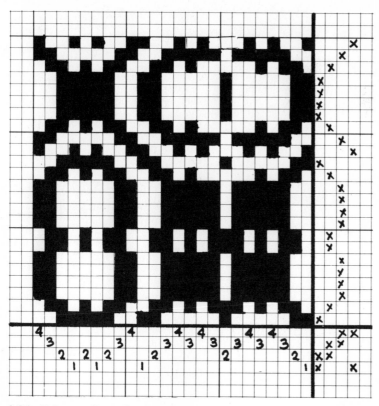

3-36. "Miniature" overshot pattern. Note the use of twill line and small block size.

3-37. Miniature overshot pattern.

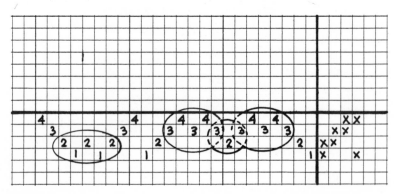

3-38. Miniature overshot pattern with blocks circled.

The number of shots follows the One-less Rule for the sections that are threaded with overshot blocks. The sections that are threaded with twill lines use one pattern shot per twill pair. The pattern is woven as-drawn-in, the shed sequence reflecting the threading draft. This pattern has a total number of twenty-four ends in the entire pattern repeat, so the pattern is only two inches long if the warp is set at twelve ends per inch. This is indeed miniature in comparison with other overshot patterns. (Compare this pattern size with some of the patterns in chapter 4.)

Many overshot patterns can be reduced to miniature size. Figure 3-39 gives a draft diagram for a wheel motif drafted in the miniature style. Here the alternation forming the top and bottom arcs of the circle is done with blocks containing the minimum number of ends; they are drafted here on blocks C and D, with three ends in each. The C and D at the beginning of the draft,

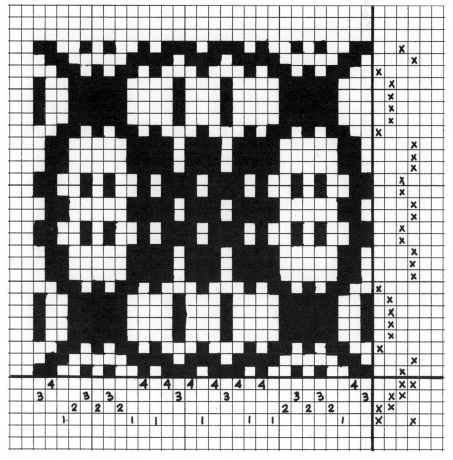

3-39. Wheel motif drafted as a miniature pattern.

forming the side arcs, are threaded with a twill line (3,4,1 and 1,4,3). The connection arcs here are not two-block alternations, but rather a five-end B block. When woven as-drawn-in, a small circle results. This pattern uses only twenty-nine threads, compared with the wheel in figure 3-29, which uses sixty-two ends.

Miniatures are useful patterns for several reasons. Since the size of the float is small, the finished fabric is more practical than one having the larger overshot blocks. The fabric can then be used where practicality is important, for instance for upholstery fabric. Miniatures are also useful for borders on fabrics where a small border is wanted.

THE SAMPLER

Practice, practice, practice! This classic line is as true for mastery of weaving as it is for any other activity. A sampler provides a place to practice and to apply your overshot knowledge. An overshot sampler is given here, but samplers can be used to study other things: color, pattern weaves, or yarn types, for example. The sampler is structured so that the various possibilities and varieties (of motifs or colors or yarn types) are all included in the threading of the warp; these are then woven off in the same order that they are threaded, much like as-drawn-in weaving.

In this overshot sampler, the motifs are threaded in such a way that, when woven, they develop in the woven piece on a diagonal, beginning in the lower right-hand corner (see fig. 3-40). Wherever the threading of a motif intersects with the treadling of a motif, the motif is seen woven in the sampler. How the treadling of one motif affects another motif can also be seen. For example, in figure 3-40, in the lower right-hand corner of the area that would usually show the draw-down, the table threading has been treadled according to the as-drawn-in table format. In the second-from-the-right square (indicated by an asterisk), the woven pattern would show what happens to a star threading when it is treadled according to the table format.

This information can be used for designing overshot patterns, because these patterns usually consist of several motifs or pattern areas. When planning them, therefore, there are two areas to be considered (among other things, such as size, function, etc.). One is the as-drawn-in areas, where the actual motif or variation will be woven. The second area is where the other threadings will be woven according to the first motif's treadling, as in the star-table example in the sampler. So it is important not only to know what the motifs look like when woven but also to understand the interaction between the various motifs and treadlings.

The threading draft of the sampler is given in figure 3-41. It includes all the basic motifs presented in this chapter. Between the threading of each motif

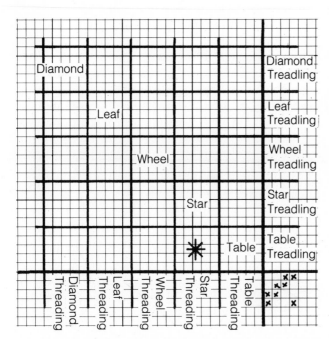

3-40. Format of sampler, showing the threading and parallel treadling.

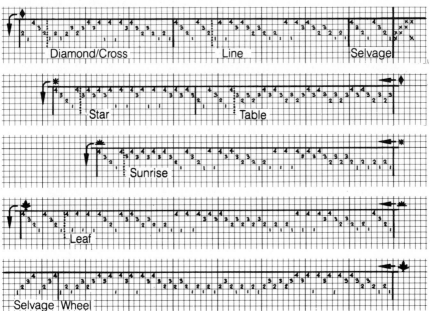

3-41. Threading diagram of the overshot sampler. The threading is read from right to left, starting in the upper right-hand corner. A dotted line separates the motif from the twill threading that is used to separate the motifs.

(and at both selvages), a twill line is threaded; the exact threading of the twill line depends on the threading of the motifs it is separating. Thus, if a motif ends with a 1, the twill line continues 2,3,4,1,2,3,4. If the motif ends with 4, the twill line starts with a 1, and so on. (The motifs can be separated in other ways. If you have a multiharness loom, for example, the ends separating the motifs can be threaded alternately on harnesses 5 and 6 and tied up to the tabby treadles, i.e., 1–3–5, and 2–4–6.) The tie-up (fig. 3-42) is given for both counterbalanced and jack looms. The treadling (which follows in the text) is given in terms of the shed that is to be opened. That is, the treadling is not stated as 1,2,3,4 (meaning treadle numbers); rather, the directions are stated as 1–2, 2–3, 3–4, or 4–1, meaning shed openings. The treadling is given motif by motif, including the treadling according to the One-less Rule as well as some variations. Tabby is not shown in the treadling sequence, but *must be woven* in actual practice.

3-42. Tie-up for overshot sampler, showing both jack and counterbalanced tie-ups.

The sampler was woven using 3/12 wool worsted for the warp, set at twelve ends per inch; this yarn was also used for the tabby weft. The pattern weft is a 2-ply wool at 1000 yards per pound. The warp and tabby weft is off-white. The pattern weft is several different colors; a different color was used with each horizontal section to set off the different motifs.

There is a total of 319 ends in the sampler; with a 12 ends per inch sley, this gives a width of 26 2/3 inches. There is no absolute length for the warp; however, I encourage you to wind one that is long enough to weave a sampler with much experimentation and many variations (including the ones in chapter 5). I suggest a minimum of two yards of weaving length, plus take-up and loom waste.

Figure 3-43 shows the sampler as I wove it, but your sampler may not be identical. Many factors will affect the finished piece: the yarns you select; the tension of the warp as you weave (I tend toward a lot of tension); how hard your beat is (here I lean toward the medium); and, of course, the exact treadlings you use. I suggest that you try the treadlings according to the One-less Rule, but use your judgment with the suggested variations. For example, if the motif when first woven according to the One-less Rule is too tall, perhaps you might

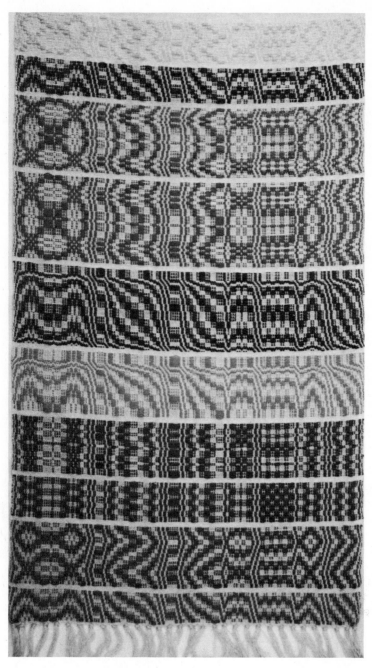

3-43. The woven sampler.

try it again with fewer shots per pattern block; for a flattened motif, adding some shots is appropriate.

Between each horizontal treadling section, there are six shots of plain weave (use the tabby weft). This separates the sections a little but is narrow enough to allow you to visualize how the motifs and variations look next to each other (as in a finished piece without separations). I have also started the sampler with three shots of plain weave, using the tabby yarn, as I do all my coverlets.

Each horizontal section is woven with a different color yarn; this helps to separate the motif sections. The colors also add interest to the piece—making it more than just a weaving exercise—and lots of cheerfulness to wherever it hangs. And now, the treadlings:

LINE:	Shed	# of Shots
	1–2	3
	2–3	3
	3–4	3
	4–1	3
	Repeat	Repeat

This completes one line section, but it can be treadled as many times as desired. Now try it with four shots per shed.

CROSS:	Shed	# Shots	Diamond:	Shed	# Shots
	1–2	3		1–4	3
	2–3	3		3–4	3
	3–4	3		2–3	3
	1–4	4		1–2	4
	3–4	3		2–3	3
	2–3	3		3–4	3
	1–2	3		1–4	3

This completes the cross and diamond woven sections as-drawn-in. Also try it with four shots for all sheds, perhaps with only two shots for the turning block. Note that two motifs are woven using only one threading and two treadling sequences.

TABLE:	Shed	# Shots
	2–3	4
	3–4	4
	2–3	4
	3–4	4
	2–3	4
	3–4	4
	2–3	4

The table could be woven with three shots per shed, or add shots if the table is too short.

STAR:	*Shed*	*# Shots*
	3–4	5
	1–4	4
	3–4	2
	1–4	4
	3–4	5

Here I wove one star as-drawn-in and then another star with four shots in all sections except the center, which had only two. This makes a slight difference, but one I wanted to explore. For other star treadling variations, also see the section on Rose Treadling in chapter 5.

SUNRISE:	*Shed*	*# Shots*
	1–2	7
	2–3	5
	3–4	5
	1–4	5
	1–2	3
	2–3	3
	3–4	3
	1–4	3
	1–2	1
	2–3	1
	3–4	1
	1–4	1
	1–2	1
	2–3	1
	3–3	8

The threading and treadling for the sunrise and leaf motifs given here are for one repeat of the motif. As indicated before, these motifs are most commonly used with a mirror-image of the threading (see figs. 4-13 and 4-15).

LEAF:	*Shed*	*# Shots*
	1–2	1
	2–3	1
	3–4	1
	1–4	1
	1–2	3
	2–3	3
	3–4	3
	1–4	5
	1–2	5
	2–3	7
	3–4	5
	1–4	5

(continued)

LEAF:	Shed	# Shots
	1–2	3
	2–3	3
	3–4	3
	1–4	1
	1–2	1
	2–3	1
	3–4	1
	1–4	6

Note the difference between the leaf and the sunrise; the leaf starts narrow, swells, and then narrows again. This makes for an undulating effect that the sunrise motif is lacking.

WHEEL:	Shed	# Shots (I)	# Shots (II)
	1–2	3	2
	2–3	3	2
	3–4	3	2
	1–4	2	2
	3–4	2	2
	1–4	2	2
	3–4	3	2
	2–3	5	5
	1–2	6	5
	2–3	2	2
	1–2	6	5
	2–3	5	5
	3–4	3	2
	1–4	2	2
	3–4	2	2
	1–4	2	2
	3–4	3	2
	2–3	3	2
	1–2	3	2

As I've said before, a round wheel is hard to achieve; this is clearly demonstrated in the oval I wove with the as-drawn-in treadling. I tried again, using the number of shots listed in the second column (II) and found the second wheel to be much more satisfactory.

I also wove two additional sections to test some color ideas. One is a repeat of the straight line motif, using a heather yarn of mixed blues with lavender flecks. The heathered yarns appear to soften the geometric lines of the overshot structure. In the last section, I used an off-white pattern weft, closely matched to the warp and tabby weft. With white on white, the pattern (here the cross/diamond) becomes very muted and resembles a texture weave. Both the heather and off-white pattern yarns produce attractive fabrics—although somewhat different than the traditional overshot—with only a slight change in the yarn.

And so your (possibly) first encounter with overshot weaving is completed. I find watching the overshot weaving pattern grow with each successive shot of weft, combined with the rhythmic picking up one shuttle and putting down another, particularly enjoyable. It is not a fast weave, although the more you practice, the faster you will become. I hope you also become more adventurous. So with the remaining warp, try some or all of the variations presented in chapter 5 and your own creative ideas as well.

4. *Patterns*

Just as overshot motifs are built on blocks, so the patterns are built on motifs. Patterns that at first glance seem different and distinct prove, on closer examination, to be related through the use of similar motifs. These motifs may be of different size, the threading may have been modified, or the treadling creatively altered, but the basic similarities will remain.

Looking at traditional patterns to analyze their motifs and interactions is another useful tool in the study of overshot. But the number and variety of traditional overshot patterns are probably greater than the number of weavers who produced them; thus, only seven patterns of the many are included here. I chose patterns that are representative of the motifs and that demonstrate their use as the building blocks of the patterns. I also looked for patterns that are well known; as you continue your weaving practice and investigation, you will be able to recognize and will become familiar with them. You should be aware, however, that the same pattern is often called by several names; some of the variety of names and their sources will be given here, but the list is by no means exhaustive. I further chose patterns that lend themselves to use with the yarn and sett that has been used for the illustrations and sampler in this book.

Most patterns are presented with a complete draft and draw-down as well as with a photograph. Again, the half-tones and tabby have been eliminated in the drafts; tabby *must* be woven in actual practice. For the most part, only one repeat of each pattern is drafted, a repeat being all the motifs and interconnecting threads necessary for the pattern (a finished piece of fabric may be threaded with any number of repeats of the pattern). In the threading draft, the last thread of the last block of the repeat has been included to show the balance of the pattern. When actually threading several repeats, this thread is eliminated since it is the common thread between the last block of the repeat and the first block of the next repeat.

Putting the repeats of a pattern together to thread a piece of fabric often requires balancing the pattern repeats. For example, if a pattern consists of the alternation of a table and a star, the threading for the fabric should not start on a table and end on a star; it should be balanced to start and finish with the same motif. Or perhaps having a border is desirable for the finished piece in order to fill out extra inches or to enhance the design of the fabric. How to fit the patterns into finished weavings will be discussed in the next chapter.

DOG TRACKS

Dog Tracks is a simple pattern consisting of alternating rows of stars. (Figures 4-1 and 4-2 show one and a half repeats of this pattern. This is possible since it is a small pattern; the other patterns in this chapter and chapter 6 are generally shown with only one repeat.) One star is threaded on blocks A and B, and the other star is threaded on blocks C and D. When A and B are treadled to produce one set of stars, half-tones and plain weave will be produced in the C and D areas, and vice versa. This is a repetitive, overall, and—to me— somewhat uninteresting pattern.

This type of pattern can be found in many other sources, with some variation. For example, in *A Handweaver's Source Book*, Davison lists a pattern called Dog Tracks, but the pattern is an alternation of tables, not of stars; in her book the pattern that looks most similar to the Dog Tracks drafted here is called Snowballs. Atwater in *Shuttle-craft Book of American Handweaving* (#37, p. 157) and the Burnhams in *Keep Me Warm One Night* (pp. 226–227), on the other hand, show patterns that resemble this Dog Tracks in form and name, as does Hall in *A Book of Hand-Woven Coverlets* (p. 60).

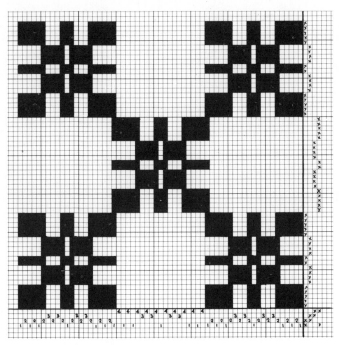

4-1. Dog Tracks pattern. This pattern has alternating rows of star motifs.

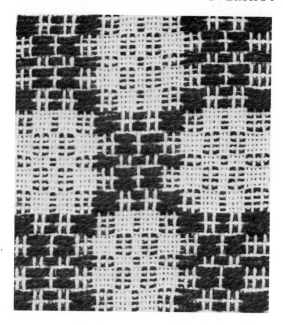

4-2. Dog tracks.

WANDERING VINE

This pattern combines the basic star figure with a number of straight lines (figs. 4-3 and 4-4). The stars are again arranged in alternating rows, as in Dog Tracks, but only two at a time and separated by straight lines, three in this case. The effect of wavy lines is formed by the elongation of the straight lines when the stars are woven and the foreshortening of the stars when the lines are woven. This type of undulating line, like the radiating motifs in chapter 3, produces strong patterns. Though one might think Wandering Vine lends itself to subtle color contrasts, one of my favorite pieces is one I wove with black as the pattern color on an off-white background.

Hall shows a similar piece in *Hand-Woven Coverlets* (p. 46), but calls it Cat Track. She also notes that names from Cat Track to Wandering Vine to Snail's Trail have been attached to this particular pattern. Davison shows two versions, both called Wandering Vine, in *Handweaver's Source Book* (p. 17) and in *Handweaver's Pattern Book* (p. 166).

ORANGE PEEL

The cross and table motifs are the basis of this pattern, but the name has clearly come from the lozenge-shaped pattern areas (figs. 4-5 and 4-6), so reminiscent of a section of peeled orange skin. The cross and table are treadled in alternation, and the lozenges are formed by the elongation of the cross when the table is treadled and the foreshortening of the table when the cross is treadled.

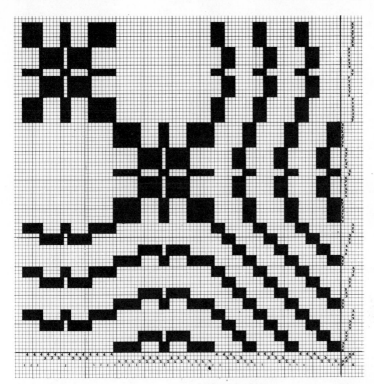

4-3. Wandering Vine pattern. This pattern has star motifs and straight lines.

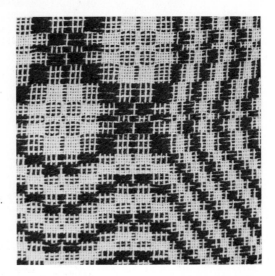

4-4. Wandering Vine.

This is one of the most popular traditional patterns and can be found in many books, in which it is usually named Orange Peel. In *Keep Me Warm One Night* (p. 188) two names are listed—The Beauty of the Lake and True Love's Vine—but the authors note that this appeared to be a very popular pattern and other names may have been used in various areas.

A variation of Orange Peel is formed by doubling the cross motif, the result

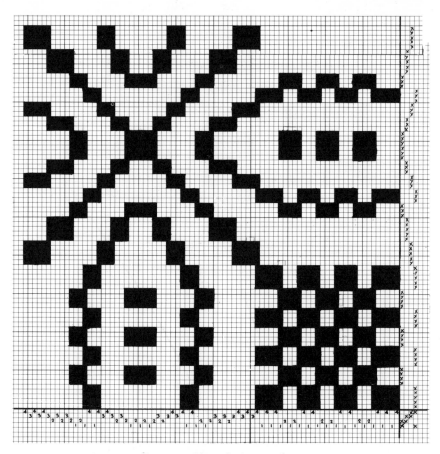

4-5. Orange Peel pattern. This uses table and cross motifs.

4-6. Orange Peel.

of which is a doubling of the lozenge figure. Atwater, in *Shuttle-craft Book of American Handweaving*, calls this variation Double Orange Peel (#10, p. 150); it is also found in A *Handweaver's Source Book* (p. 57) as Double Compass Work, and in *Keep Me Warm One Night* (p. 206) as a variation of the Canadian pattern named Monmouth.

DOUBLE CHARIOT WHEELS

This pattern is made up of a pair of stars and a table, both "fancier" versions of the basic motif (figs. 4-7 and 4-8). The stars are separated by a small cross and when woven produce the four wheellike figures, or Chariot Wheels.

Another name frequently attached to this pattern is Church Windows. In *Hand-Woven Coverlets* Hall suggests that the configuration is reminiscent of a rose window in an English cathedral, hence the name Church Windows. In *Keep Me Warm One Night* (p. 240), there is a similar pattern, but the name is Distant Beauty.

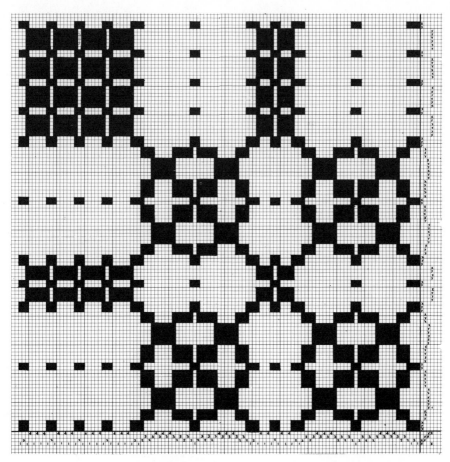

4-7. Double Chariot Wheels pattern. Star and table motifs are used.

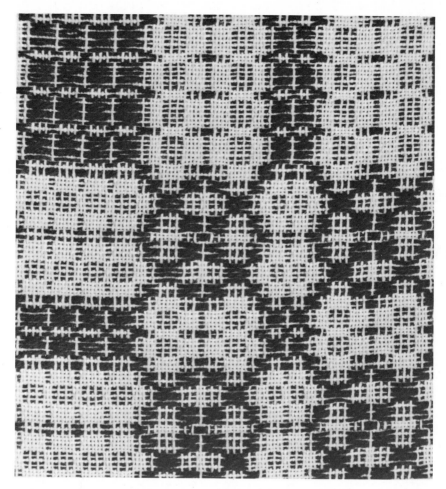

4-8. Double Chariot Wheels.

The Chariot Wheel is often used in other patterns, singled, doubled, and more. Strickler in A *Portfolio of American Coverlets* shows a coverlet with a pattern called Nine Chariot Wheels (vol. 1, #10). Atwater in *Shuttle-craft Book of American Handweaving* includes several single-wheel patterns such as Weaver Rose's Single Chariot Wheel (p. 169, #77) and Single Chariot Wheels (p. 167, #65).

YOUNG LOVER'S KNOT

This wheel pattern is undoubtedly one of the most popular and widely recognized of the Colonial patterns (figs. 4-9 and 4-10). The wheel is more detailed than in the simpler version in Chariot Wheels and is threaded like the wheel in chapter 3 (fig. 3-29). The wheels are separated here by a simple cross.

This pattern is found in many books, including Strickler, *Portfolio of American Covelets* (vol. 2, #1), Atwater *Shuttle-craft Book of American Handweaving* (p. 174, #98), and Black *New Keys to Weaving* (p. 222). In *Keep Me Warm One Night*, the same pattern is known as Single Chariot Wheel (p. 236, #313), an interesting contrast to the American tradition, which uses that name to describe patterns using the simpler wheel.

4-9. Young Lover's Knot pattern. The motifs are wheel and cross.

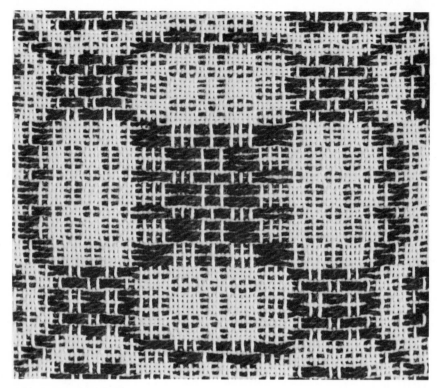

4-10. Young Lover's Knot.

The major variation of Young Lover's Knot is *Whig Rose* (fig. 4-11), a pattern that is probably even more popular and widespread than Young Lover's Knot. The Whig Rose pattern is woven by treadling the Young Lover's Knot threading in the "rose" fashion mentioned in chapter 3 (and discussed in chapter 5). The treadling is shown in figure 4-12. In Whig Rose, the five rose figures are enclosed in the circular lines, in contrast to Young Lover's Knot, where the stars form part of the wheel's perimeter. Whig Rose also shows interlocking circles, unlike the discrete ones in Young Lover's Knot.

SUNRISE

There are many patterns that use radiating lines to form the sunrise configuration. The one chosen for inclusion here shows the parallel lines radiating from a central block, alternating with a group of four small tables separated by a cross (fig. 4-13). The cross is accentuated at the ends and center by a larger block than is found in the rest of the cross.

Only the threading is given for this pattern and for the next, Double Bow Knot. The rest of the draft diagram is left for you to do as an exercise. Use the standard tie-up (see fig. 3-42). Because this pattern is woven as-drawn-in, the treadling sequence reflects the threading sequence. If you choose to do the draw-down for yourself, start with a large sheet of graph paper, or smaller sheets taped together. The pattern has 206 ends in a repeat, and even with eight-to-the-inch graph paper the total draw-down would be longer than 25 inches on each side. The threading is given in figure 4-14. The numbers (or ends) in figure 4-14 should be transferred to your own graph paper, with the first number in the upper right becoming the first number of the threading section of your draft diagram. Follow the threading sequence right to left and down the page.

4-11. Whig Rose. This is the Young Lover's Knot pattern treadled rose fashion.

Whig Rose		Young Lover's Knot	
1-2	2x	1-4	2x
1-4	3x	1-2	3x
3-4	3x	2-3	3x
2-3	4x	3-4	4x
3-4	3x	2-3	3x
1-4	3x	1-2	3x
1-2	3x	1-4	3x
2-3	3x	3-4	3x
3-4	4x	2-3	4x
2-3	4x	3-4	4x
3-4	4x	2-3	4x
2-3	3x	3-4	3x
1-2	7x	1-4	7x
1-4	6x	1-2	6x
1-2	2x	1-4	2x
1-4	2x	1-2	2x
1-2	2x	1-4	2x
1-4	6x	1-2	6x
1-2	7x	1-4	7x
2-3	3x	3-4	3x
3-4	4x	2-3	4x
2-3	4x	3-4	4x
3-4	4x	2-3	4x
2-3	3x	3-4	3x
1-2	3x	1-4	3x
1-4	3x	1-2	3x
3-4	3x	2-3	3x
2-3	4x	3-4	4x
3-4	3x	2-3	3x
1-4	3x	1-2	3x
1-2	2x	1-4	2x

4-12. Shed sequences for Young Lover's Knot and Whig Rose.

This pattern can be found by the same name in *Hand-Woven Coverlets* (p. 250), and is noted to be similar to one called Jefferson's Fancy. It is also in *Keep Me Warm One Night* (p. 195, #249) where, although it is not given a specific name, it is included in the Rising Sun and Sunburst type of pattern. Atwater lists eight patterns of the sunrise type in *American Handweaving* (pp. 178–180).

DOUBLE BOW KNOT

This type of pattern uses the leaf motif, in which the radiating lines are not completely parallel but instead are closed at either end, forming a leaf figure

4-13. Sunrise pattern. This uses the radiating motif.

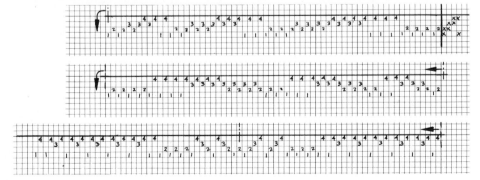

4-14. Threading draft of Sunrise pattern.

(fig. 4-15). The pattern presented here shows a pair of leaves mirrored around a central block, creating a four-leaf figure; it is combined with a large, plain table. As mentioned before, with both types of radiating patterns, a table is a good choice for a complementary motif. The radiating patterns are strong and vivid, so that combining them with a simple motif usually works best. The threading sequence for this pattern is given in figure 4-16.

Many variations, and even more names, are possible with this type of pattern. Atwater has drafts for eleven leaf-type patterns (*Shuttle-craft Book of American Handweaving*, pp. 180–183). One eye-dazzling variation is called Turkey

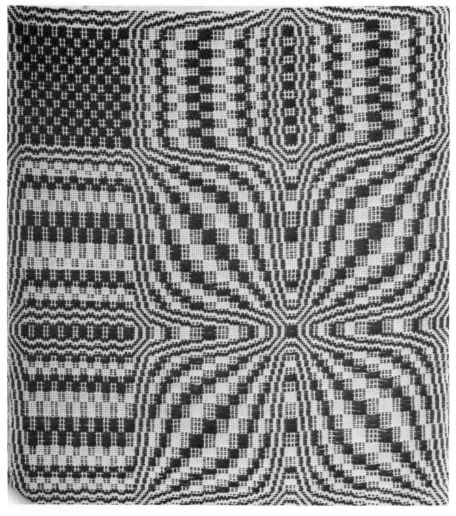

4-15. Double Bow Knot. This pattern consists of radiating leaf motifs.

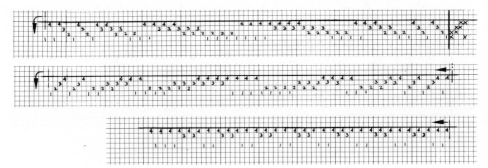

4-16. Threading draft of Double Bow Knot.

Tracks in *Keep Me Warm One Night* (p. 197, #252); here alternating motifs have been eliminated, leaving only the vibrations of the leaf motifs. Names also abound. The Double Bow Knot, exactly as presented here, is also known as Maple Leaf or Reed Leaf or Double Muscadine Hulls according to Atwater (*Shuttle-craft Book of American Handweaving*, p. 182). Hall, in *Handwoven Coverlets*, calls this pattern Hickory Leaf (p. 6). *Keep Me Warm One Night* includes a coverlet with this pattern (p. 195, #250), but does not name it.

The patterns presented in this chapter barely scratch the surface of the multitude of traditional overshot patterns. (Chapter 6 presents twenty-five additional patterns for further experimentation with and study of overshot patterns.) Studying the patterns is interesting historically and also is a way of exploring how motif combinations form patterns. One can see how the combinations work and what effect the treadling of one motif has on another motif, much the same way as in the sampler. This knowledge is another step in working toward designing your own overshot patterns, traditional or original.

5. Variations and Original Designs

Traditional, as-drawn-in overshot has been explored through its basic structure (blocks), the block combinations (motifs), and the motif combinations (patterns). Now let us turn our attention to variations of the basic weave and to some suggestions for designing your own overshot.

DESIGNING OVERSHOT PATTERNS

Many factors are included in this creative process: yarn type, color, threadings, and treadlings, to name just a few. Some considerations and possibilities are discussed here; perhaps they will be starting points for your own flights of fancy.

Materials

The type of warp and weft yarns that are chosen, as with all weaving, will influence the appearance and texture of the finished piece. In overshot there are three yarns to be chosen: warp, tabby weft, and pattern weft. The warp yarn, as with other pattern structures and weaves, must be selected with strength in mind first, so that the yarn can withstand the tension of the warping process and subsequent weaving. In overshot, this warp yarn is usually the tabby weft yarn as well. A relatively soft pattern weft yarn works best with traditional overshot so that the floats will pack down into the tabby background. Harder, stiffer yarns will tend to distort the pattern because they do not pack down as well. Smooth yarns will generally enhance the pattern; fuzzy yarns will tend to mask it, although this is one variation to consider. I have woven overshot with mohair and other fuzzy yarns and have been pleased with the results. The pattern looks softer and less geometric, an interesting contrast. Experiment with your own yarn preferences, too, especially with pattern weft yarns.

The size of the warp yarn is another important consideration, since it will determine the sett and the sett influences the length of the floats. Colonial era coverlets were usually woven with fine yarns, with twenty to forty ends per inch. This meant that a block could have ten to twenty ends in it and still only produce a 1/2-inch float. My own preferences led me to work primarily with warp yarns of approximately 2,000 yards per pound, set at twelve ends per inch; this means that any block with more than six ends will have a 1/2-

inch or longer float. This is a limiting factor since many traditional patterns have large blocks; I find I have to adapt most traditional patterns for reproduction. In designing my own patterns, I have used blocks containing up to nine ends, but keep in mind that this will produce a piece of weaving with limited practicality: the longer float will snag more easily and wear out more quickly. If you prefer, try the finer yarns, or use the heavier yarns with their limitations; I have had no complaints about the durability of my weavings, but keep in mind that, if it is an heirloom you wish to create, two hundred years from now your coverlet may not be around.

Traditionally, the same yarn and the same color are used for the warp and tabby weft. But color is another area for experimentation; you might consider trying a different color for the tabby weft, or several different colors in the warp or the weft. (See Alternate Treadlings and Other Variations.)

Structure and Layout

The structure of the blocks on which the various motifs are drafted affect the appearance of the pattern. As stated earlier, it is not the actual blocks that define the motif, but rather the format of the combination of the blocks. Thus, a table can be drafted on blocks A and B, or on C and D, and so on; the table will look the same, although the actual threading is different (compare figs. 3-1 and 3-3). However, the patterns (or motif combinations) are affected by the specific blocks used in the motifs. For example, a pattern with tables on A and B alternating with stars on C and D (fig. 5-1) will be similar but not identical to a pattern with a table on A and B and stars on B and C (fig. 5-2). In figure 5-1, the motifs are more separate; in figure 5-2, there is an extra set of blocks outlining the table. This outline results from the B block, which is part of the structure of both the table and the star. The B block, then, is woven as part of the table and as part of the star. The pattern in figure 5-1 is crisper and the tables more clearly defined as a result.

The layout is another factor in the appearance of the pattern. With overshot patterns, the layout is primarily of the overall type, with small motifs and repeats such as Dog Tracks (fig. 4-1), or larger repeats such as Double Bow Knot (fig. 4-15). The motifs can be of relatively equal size, as with Dog Tracks, which has same-sized stars in alternating rows. They can also be unequal, as with Sunrise (fig. 4-13), where the radiating lines are much larger than the table pattern area.

Borders can be planned with overall patterns to vary the appearance of the piece. This can add interest to an otherwise repetitive pattern, Dog Tracks, for example. The border can be the outer part of the pattern, or it can be set into the pattern threading. Figures 5-3 and 5-4 give the threading outlines of these layouts.

There are several ways to plan threading drafts for borders. A very easy plan

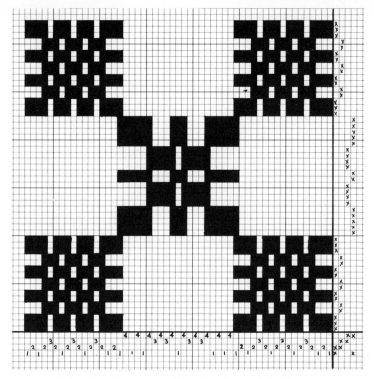

5-1. Draft diagram of pattern with A–B tables and C–D stars, showing more discrete motifs.

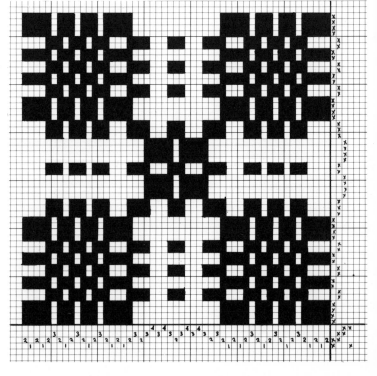

5-2. Draft diagram of pattern with A–B tables and B–C stars, showing extra set of blocks around table.

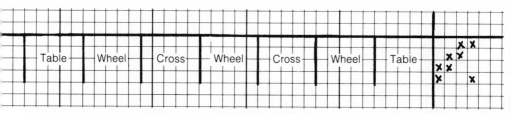

5-3. Threading layout showing border at outer edges of weaving.

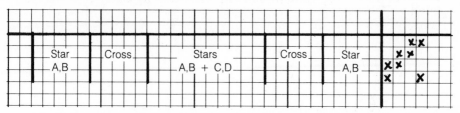

5-4. Threading layout showing border set slightly into pattern.

is to thread several rows of straight lines of overshot blocks. This is a safe choice that will blend well with many patterns, particularly elaborate ones; it is not a very interesting choice, however. Diamonds are also good with many patterns and are frequently seen in borders. They are somewhat more interesting than the straight lines.

Another method that is often used for border threading is to choose part of the pattern draft and use it for the border. For example, to make a border for Orange Peel (fig. 4-5), the center of the cross threading might be chosen. This is threaded D,C,B,A,B,C,D, with the central A block larger than the others; the threading could be repeated two or three times at each edge to form a border.

Or you might want to use another motif altogether in the border. This method is one that requires great care in the selection of the motif. Your sampler can be especially useful here in choosing a motif that will interact well with the rest of the pattern (even with this help, however, some of your choices will work and some will not). An example of this type of border threading is given in figure 5-5, where a table border is threaded with a wheel and cross pattern draft.

In general, if the pattern has large and complex repeats in it, a simple, small border will probably be best; if the pattern is small and repetitive, then a more intricate border can be tried. Like all other aspects of designing, practice and experimentation are necessary to develop skill in selecting good borders.

Designing on Paper

Designing overshot patterns can be approached in several ways (but do not get discouraged if your first designs do not work out exactly as hoped for). One

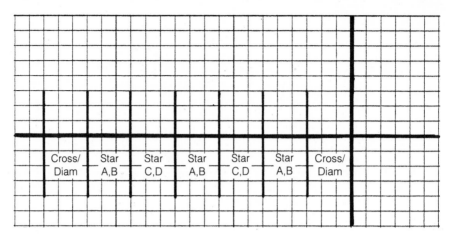

5-5. Threading layout showing border threaded with different motif than pattern.

method is to select motifs and put them together in various ways, using the sampler or other patterns as a guide. This method, especially at first, is a trial-and-error process, but one that, with practice, can be fruitful and fun. It is very important to draw-down these trials to see exactly how the motifs balance each other and work together. This process can mean many hours of filling in squares on graph paper, but using a shorthand draft form can reduce some of those tedious hours of work. Let us digress briefly and explore this shorthand draft. It is called a *profile draft*; each square of the graph represents several ends instead of one end. Figure 5-6 shows a profile draft of the cross/diamond in figure 3-1.

The profile draft can be useful but presents some problems. In a weave structure in which each block contains a consistent number of ends (like summer and winter), each square can represent one block; but in overshot, a block theoretically can contain three to any number of ends. Also, all blocks except turning blocks have an even number of threads in them, so that either the turning blocks or the straight progression blocks are not precisely represented. Let's look at a specific example.

Figure 3-1 gives the draft for a simple cross/diamond, and figure 5-6 shows the same draft in profile form. Here each square of the graph represents two ends; this allows for the greatest flexibility but is the least time-saving. Note that the turning block in figure 3-1 has five ends in it, but is represented in the profile draft with three squares. You must choose whether to make the turning block larger or smaller than indicated by the profile draft in order to achieve the uneven number of ends necessary for turning blocks. In the previous example, the three squares of the profile draft represented only five ends in the actual threading draft.

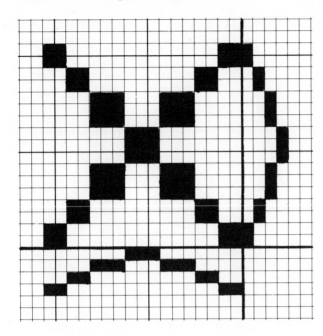

5-6. Profile draft of cross/diamond threading given in figure 3-1.

If each square represents four ends, then of course the shorthand draft saves more time. However, in terms of overshot threadings, the choices are more limited. There are many six-thread or ten-thread blocks that could not be represented easily in profile drafts where each square equals four ends. Thus, while profile drafting is somewhat of a shortcut to filling in graph squares in draw-downs, it is not an easy fit with overshot weaving and must be used with care and discretion.

The profile draft can be useful in designing overshot threadings when a pattern is first made on graph paper and block names assigned to the pattern areas, and then a threading is worked out. This process is shown in figures 5-7 and 5-8. On graph paper, squares are filled in to make a profile pattern (fig. 5-7), then the rows are given block names. The first line of floats are called block A, with two repeats of this block each time it appears. The next line is called block B, with only one repeat; the third line is a repeat of the first line and thus is also an A row. The next row is named D (C cannot follow A), followed by C, then B, C, and D (each of these rows has only one repeat of the block in it). This ends the repeat; the beginning set of blocks (A,B,A) is shown for balance. The threading draft (fig. 5-8) is then made from the assigned blocks. In making this threading draft, each square in the profile draft is taken to represent a four-thread block. The tie-up will be the standard overshot tie-up, and the treadling can be anything from traditional, as-drawn-in to some of the variations possible.

5-7. Profile pattern. Squares are filled in on graph paper to make an original pattern.

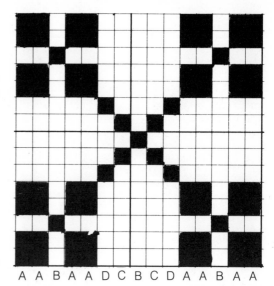

5-8. Threading draft based on profile pattern in figure 5-7.

A A B A A D C B C D A A B A A

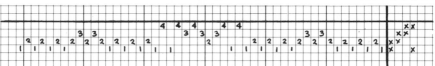

Balancing the Pattern

Having decided on a layout, or a pattern, to be used, work out the total threading draft. This will include the repeats of the pattern, borders if applicable, and the selvages. Selvages are added so that the edges of the finished fabric will be even. The selvage for overshot is usually one or more lines of straight twill on both sides of the warp.

The repeats of the pattern need to be balanced for symmetry around the center. The warp should be threaded to begin and end with the same motif, regardless of how many repeats of each motif or pattern element are planned. Thus a pattern of wheels and crosses may be threaded as follows: cross, wheel, cross, wheel, cross. Or there may be more wheels and crosses, but the initial and ending motif will be a cross.

When joining several pieces of fabric to make coverlets or other large weavings, the total piece should be balanced around the center, but the individual pieces do not have to be. For example, using wheels and crosses again, the threading draft might be arranged: wheel, cross, wheel, cross, wheel, half a cross. Two pieces are then woven, and a seam joining the pieces is made at the half-cross side of the warp. Two lines of twill are used as a selvage at the wheel side, but four or five lines are used at the half-cross side for a seam allowance. When sewn together, the two half crosses meet to form a single cross. The large fabric is symmetrical and balanced, although the individual strips are not.

Figuring out the correct number of ends and threading the loom correctly can be difficult at first. A chart that I use to help keep track of the threads and motifs, both for record keeping and for actually threading the loom, is presented in Appendix A.

ALTERNATE TREADLINGS AND OTHER VARIATIONS

Designing an original overshot threading and pattern is quite a challenge, especially for the novice. To achieve variety, there are alternate methods for weaving overshot threadings; some will result in woven pieces that are similar to as-drawn-in overshot, and some will produce very different fabrics. These alternate treadlings and weaving methods can be used with traditional patterns or with your own designs, and different appearing pieces can be woven on one warp and threading.

Rose Treadling

One of the most widely known treadling variations is the rose-star conversion; this was previously mentioned in the description of the star motif and the Young Lover's Knot pattern. Weaving star fashion is another way of saying weaving as-drawn-in. To weave motifs as-drawn-in (or star fashion), the blocks of the motif are treadled in the order that they are threaded. To weave rose fashion, the treadling order is inverted. For example, if a star is drafted A,B,A,B,A, it would be treadled A,B,A,B,A to weave as-drawn-in, and B,A,B,A,B to weave rose fashion. This is not weaving the opposite of blocks A and B (blocks C and D) but rather inverting the order of the sheds.

Whig Rose and Young Lover's Knot are shown in figures 5-9 and 5-10 for comparison. The threading draft for both is the same as the one given for Young Lover's Knot in figure 4-9; the shed sequence for each is shown in figure 5-11. Note how the rose treadling affects the other pattern elements; in Young Lover's Knot the circles are separate, and in Whig Rose they interlock. Try weaving the sampler star motifs in rose fashion, and see how the other areas of the sampler are affected.

Honeycomb

Overshot threadings woven rose fashion still look like traditional overshot. Other variations and treadlings result in fabrics quite unlike the classic overshot; honeycomb is one of these (fig. 5-12). It is a weaving method, and can be used with other weave structures also. In honeycomb, heavy- and fine-weight yarns are used to achieve a textured effect of "dimples" outlined with heavy

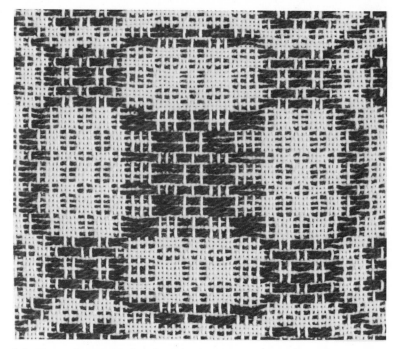

5-9. Young Lover's Knot. This wheel and cross pattern is threaded as-drawn-in.

5-10. Whig Rose. This is the Young Lover's Knot pattern woven rose fashion.

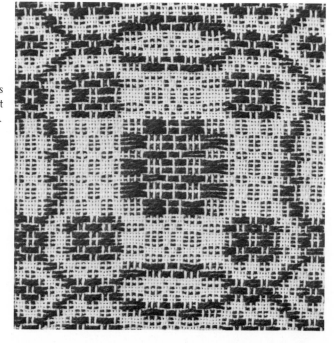

5-11. Shed sequence for Young Lover's Knot and Whig Rose.

Whig Rose		Young Lover's Knot	
1-2	2x	1-4	2x
1-4	3x	1-2	3x
3-4	3x	2-3	3x
2-3	4x	3-4	4x
3-4	3x	2-3	3x
1-4	3x	1-2	3x
1-2	3x	1-4	3x
2-3	3x	3-4	3x
3-4	4x	2-3	4x
2-3	4x	3-4	4x
3-4	4x	2-3	4x
2-3	3x	3-4	3x
1-2	7x	1-4	7x
1-4	6x	1-2	6x
1-2	2x	1-4	2x
1-4	2x	1-2	2x
1-2	2x	1-4	2x
1-4	6x	1-2	6x
1-2	7x	1-4	7x
2-3	3x	3-4	3x
3-4	4x	2-3	4x
2-3	4x	3-4	4x
3-4	4x	2-3	4x
2-3	3x	3-4	3x
1-2	3x	1-4	3x
1-4	3x	1-2	3x
3-4	3x	2-3	3x
2-3	4x	3-4	4x
3-4	3x	2-3	3x
1-4	3x	1-2	3x
1-2	2x	1-4	2x

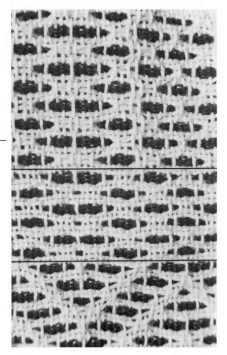

5-12. Honeycomb weaving, showing three types of treadling.

lines. The warp and the heavy-weight yarns are usually the same color. The
fine-weight yarn, which forms the dimple, is a contrasting color; this enhances
the textural effect. The effect is further heightened by using threadings in which
the blocks contain a relatively large number of ends. Honeycomb is treadled
with pairs of tabby shots (*a* and *b*) alternating with pattern shots, as below:

Shed	Yarn
a	heavy
b	heavy
1	fine ⎫
2	fine ⎭ as many shots as desired
b	heavy
a	heavy
3	fine ⎫
4	fine ⎭ as many shots as desired

Here the tabby is treadled a,b, first and then b,a; if treadled only a,b or b,a
consistently, the effect of the honeycomb is lessened. The twill pairs can be
woven with the fine-weight yarn shots, instead of with the opposite pairs of 1
and 2, or 3 and 4, as above. The treadling would then be:

Shed	Yarn
a	heavy
b	heavy
1	fine ⎫
2	fine ⎭ as many shots as desired
b	heavy
a	heavy
2	fine ⎫
3	fine ⎭ as many shots as desired
a	heavy
b	heavy
3	fine ⎫
4	fine ⎭ as many shots as desired
b	heavy
a	heavy
4	fine ⎫
1	fine ⎭ as many shots as desired

Figure 5-12 shows the results of using the honeycomb weaving method with
an overshot threading. The threading is a Goose Eye-type overshot; a draft
diagram of this is shown in figure 5-13. The top part of the photograph shows
the treadling method using the 1 and 2 sheds, and then the 3 and 4 sheds,

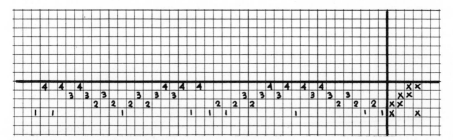

5-13. Goose Eye Overshot threading draft diagram.

with the a,b and b,a tabby alternation. Below this is a section woven with the same fine-weight sheds, but using an a,b tabby throughout. The bottom section shows the twill treadling (using the 1 and 2, then 2 and 3, then 3 and 4, then 4 and 1 sheds) with the a,b and b,a tabby alternating. Each section has its own appearance, one that is quite different from the appearance of as-drawn-in overshot.

Boundweave

Boundweave is another treadling variation, like honeycomb, that can be woven with several weave structures, including overshot. It makes use of the concept of *opposites*, that is, of combinations without common elements. Boundweave is woven without tabby and produces a weft-faced fabric that is quite dissimilar to traditional overshot.

Weft-faced fabrics range from the weft being somewhat more predominant than the warp, to the weft completely covering and obscuring the warp. With boundweave, if the warp is to be completely covered, the sett of the warp must be wider than for as-drawn-in overshot (e.g., eight ends per inch as opposed to twelve ends per inch). With the denser twelve-ends-per-inch sley, a weft-faced fabric can be woven, but the warp will not be completely covered.

The simplest type of boundweaving uses a straight progression of the overshot pairs, but instead of each shot being followed by a shot of tabby, each pattern shot is followed by a shot of the opposite pair; tabby is not woven. Thus a treadling might be: 1–2, 3–4, 2–3, 1–4, 3–4, 1–2, 1–4, 2–3. Two colors are used in alternation, one for the pattern shots and one for the opposites shots. An example of boundweave is shown in figure 5-14, woven on the Goose Eye threading draft in figure 5-13.

Both the color sequence and the treadling sequence can be varied. The *Italian* fashion of boundweave uses a three-shot sequence: a pattern shot, a shot of the adjacent pair to the pattern shot, and a shot of the pair opposite to the adjacent pair. An example of the shed sequence is 1–2, 2–3, 1–4; 2–3, 3–4, 1–2; 3–4, 1–4, 2–3; and so on. The three shots can be repeated as many times as desired to build up a unit of pattern (like the blocks in as-drawn-in

5-14. Boundweave. This treadling method produces weft-faced fabric.

overshot). Before moving on to the next three shot sequence, one shot of the first pair in the sequence is thrown. A partial treadling might be: 1–2, 2–3, 1–4, 1–2, 2–3, 1–4, 1–2, 2–3, 1–4, 1–2; 2–3, 3–4, 1–2, and so on. Three colors, or different shades of one color, are used in the same order throughout, the first color for the pattern shots, the second color for the adjacent shots, and the third color for the opposites shots. Thus the units start and end with the same color. The Italian-fashion weaving is shown in figure 5-15, using the Goose Eye threading in figure 5-13.

5-15. Italian fashion weaving. In this treadling method, weft-faced fabric with a specific color sequence is produced.

In *flamepoint* weaving, four colors or different shades of one color are used, and the treadling sequence is a straight progression of the overshot pairs, with no tabby and no opposites in between. The colors are used, in order, as many times as desired. The sequence of color then shifts so that the last color becomes the first for the desired number of shots. This is accomplished by weaving two shots in a row with the first color; this is done each time a color shift is desired. Flamepoint is shown in figure 5-16, using the same Goose Eye threading.

5-16. Flamepoint weaving. This treadling method produces weft-faced fabric with a specific color sequence.

Color Variations

Color variations, such as the ones discussed above with boundweaving, can be used with as-drawn-in overshot weaving. Perhaps different blocks or motifs could be woven with wefts of different colors; care must be taken here or the finished fabric can be stripey-looking. For example, using Dog Tracks, the A-B stars could be one color or shade and the C-D stars another. Or perhaps different colors or shades could be used within each block, as with the Italian and flamepoint methods. This can be subtle, with shades of one color, or flamboyant, with contrasting colors. Try these variations on the sampler also.

The warp color can be varied too. The warp can be more than one color, either randomly or coordinated with the threading (e.g., all wheels blue, all crosses white). The tabby weft color can then be one of the warp colors, or different colors in different sections, or perhaps another color altogether.

Opposites

All of the overshot described thus far involved threading the blocks in an adjacent manner, so that adjacent blocks have an element in common with the preceding block. With this variation, opposites threading, not only the treadling sequence but the actual threading structure are altered. With an opposites threading, the blocks do not have this common element; in a straight progression, block A (1,2) is followed by block C (3,4) instead of B (2,3) or D (1,4). An example of this is shown in figure 5-17, using the opposites blocks of A and C. Although tabby has been eliminated from the draft diagram as before, it must be woven here. There are no half-tones in two-block opposites,

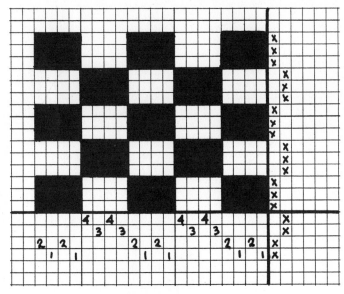

5-17. Two-block opposites with equal-sized blocks.

since there are no common elements. Variety is introduced into two-block opposites threadings by using blocks of different sizes, as in figures 5-18 and 5-19. These two-block overshot opposites patterns are known as *monk's belt*.

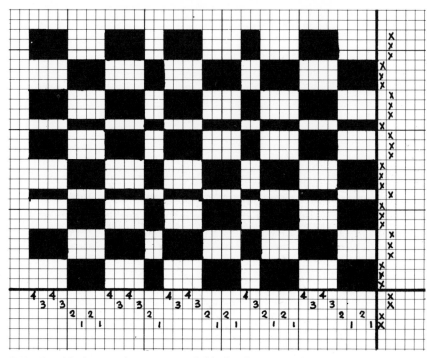

5-18. Two-block opposites pattern, with blocks of varying sizes; also known as Monk's Belt.

It is also possible to weave using four-block overshot opposites threadings; an example is given in figures 5-20 and 5-21. With four-block opposites, the half-tones are not eliminated completely but are in a different place (the half-tones are included in the draw-down in figure 5-20 to demonstrate this). All four overshot blocks are threaded, but not in an adjacent manner; that is, 1,2 is not succeeded by 2,3 or 1,4 but by the opposite block of 3,4. Because all four blocks are threaded and woven, the half-tones will appear, as they do in adjacent overshot patterns. However, the half-tones are found all together between the motifs that are being woven, not interwoven in the float area.

Another pattern element called *accidentals* is found in four-block opposites overshot. The accidentals are two-thread units in the half-tone area (half-tones are only one thread long); several of the accidentals are indicated by arrows in figure 5-20. These two-thread accidentals are formed by the transition from

5-19. Monk's Belt.

5-20. Four-block opposites pattern. The accidentals are indicated by arrows.

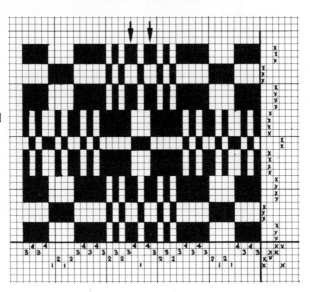

5-21. Four-block opposites pattern.

one opposites block to the next. For example, a threading in opposites from block A to block C is 1,2,1,2,3,4,3,4. Between blocks A and C, a 2 thread and a 3 thread are adjacent, forming a small B block. In four-block opposites, when the B block is woven to form the other opposites motif (on B and D), the accidentals are also woven. Accidentals also occur in the two-block opposites threading (the threading 1,2,1,2,3,4,3,4 also includes the 2-3 adjacency), but since the accidental block is never treadled or woven (only 1-2 and 3-4 are treadled, not 2-3), they are not seen.

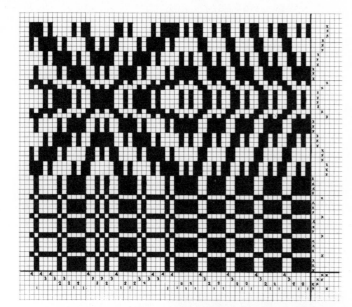

5-22. Overshot pattern with opposites and adjacent threading used together.

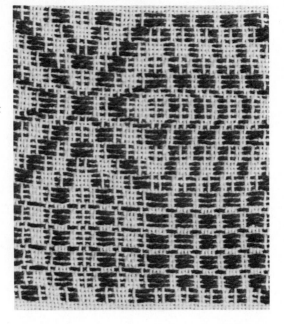

5-23. Opposites and adjacent threading overshot pattern.

Opposites and adjacent overshot can be combined in the same threading draft. This has the effect of highlighting the opposites pattern area with the cleaner lines that the opposites weaving produces. Figures 5-22 and 5-23 show an example of this type of threading. The table has been drafted on opposites and the cross with adjacent overshot threading.

6. And More Patterns

Twenty-five patterns are presented here as a resource for further study and for additional weaving practice. Some are original designs; most are adaptations of traditional patterns. They were chosen and adapted for use with a twelve-ends-per-inch sley and cover a range of overshot patterns. One pattern repeat of each pattern has been drafted (except in figs. 6-1 and 6-2); the last thread of the last block has been eliminated for ease of threading, since it will be the first thread in the first block of the next repeat. (See Balancing the Pattern in chapter 5, and Appendix A, for information on using the repeat to make a pattern plan.)

The patterns are arranged in order by the size of the pattern repeat, starting with some miniatures. The size of the pattern repeat is a help in choosing a pattern for a particular fabric. The larger patterns clearly will not be as useful for smaller pieces of fabric or for border treadlings; they will work best with larger coverlets or wallhangings. One repeat of the larger patterns (with a partial repeat for balance) can be used for pillow or placemat threadings. The smaller repeats, which can be boringly repetitive in a larger piece, can be woven where overall patterns are desired, such as for smaller coverlets, afghans, or baby blankets.

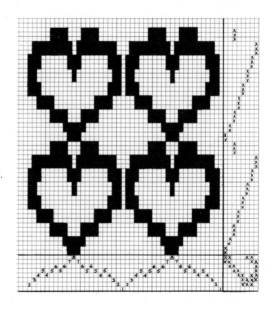

6-1. Hearts
(two repeats).

6-2. Honeysuckle (two repeats).

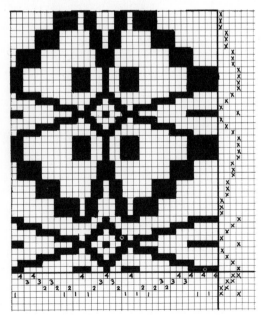

6-3. Maltese Cross.

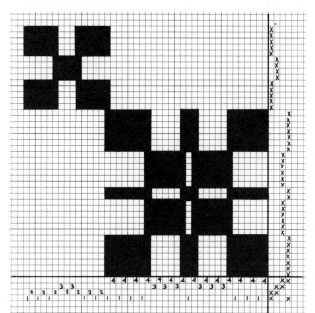

6-4. Sweet Briar Beauty.

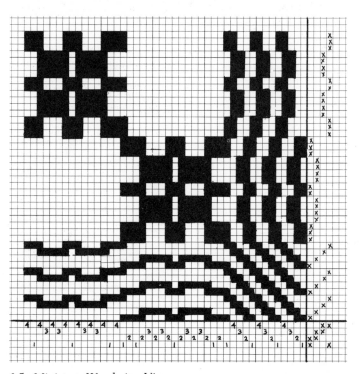

6-5. Miniature Wandering Vine.

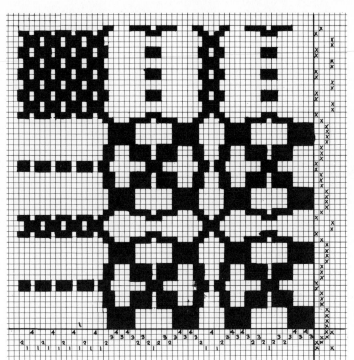

6-6. Miniature Chariot Wheels.

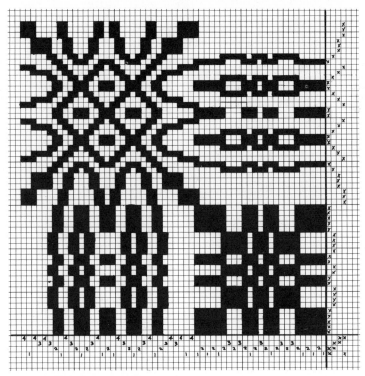

6-7. Double Orange Peel.

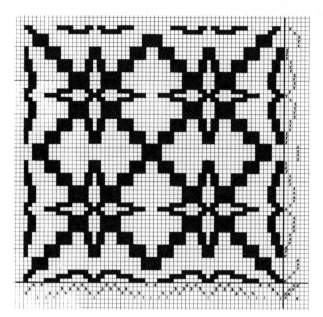

6-8. Carol's Design.

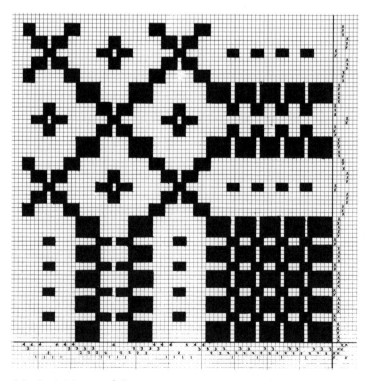

6-9. Sun, Moon and Stars.

6-10. Wheel of Fortune.

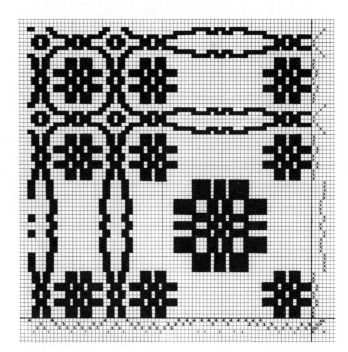

6-11. Wreath Rose.

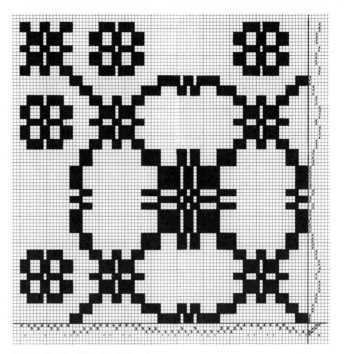

6-12. Single Chariot Wheel.

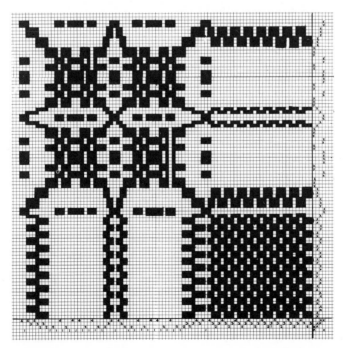

6-13. Star Dance.

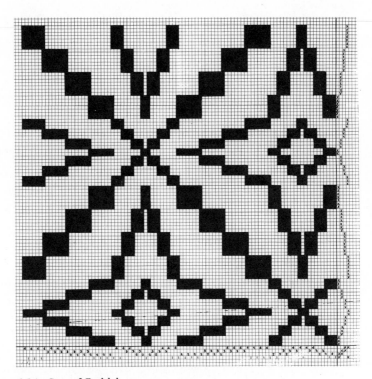

6-14. Star of Bethlehem.

6-15. Miniature Bow Knot.

6-16. Rose/Knot.

6-17. Cloudless
Beauty.

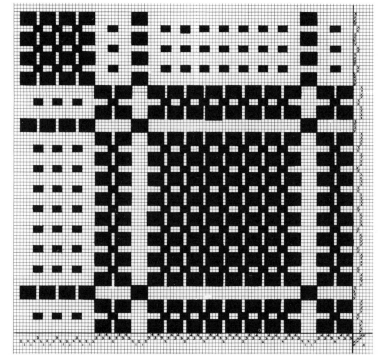

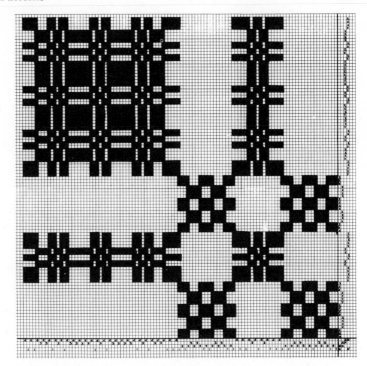

6-18. All Stars.

6-19. Blooming Sunburst.

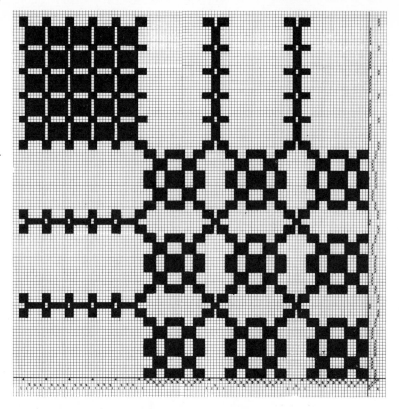

6-20. The Nine Roses.

6-21. Velvet Rose

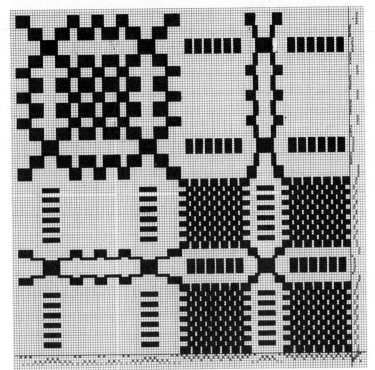

6-22. Plum Pattern.

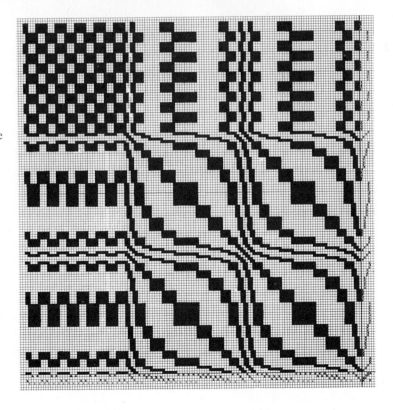

6-23. Panache Pattern.

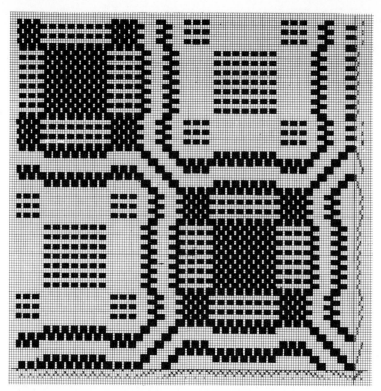

6-24. Sunflower.

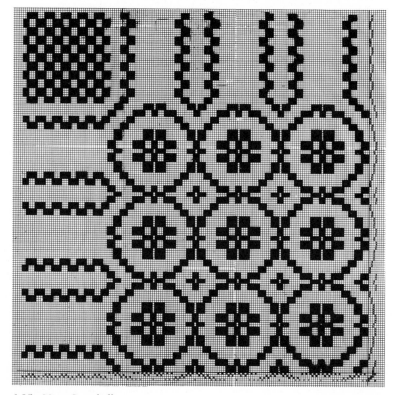

6-25. Nine Snowballs.

Appendix A:
Record-keeping/
Warping Chart

This is a chart I use to help keep track of the many warp ends needed for a coverlet and also to keep records of my work. I break down each motif (or pattern area) into the number of threads used per harness, then multiply this number by the number of repeats of the motif, and keep totals for each harness and for each motif.

DOG TRACKS

HARNESS	Selvage ×4	Star1 ×8	Star2 ×7		Totals per Harness
4	1	0	10	number of threads per single motif per harness	
	4	0	70	number of threads per total number of motifs per harness	74
3	1	4	4		
	4	32	28		64
2	1	10	0		
	4	80	0		84
1	1	7	5		
	4	56	35		95
Single Motif Total	4	21	19		
Multiple Motif Total	16	168	133		317
	Total Piece: // + 7(S1 + S2) + S1 + //				

The example given here is based on the threading draft for Dog Tracks (fig. 4-1), a pattern with alternating rows of stars. I planned seven repeats of the pattern, a repeat of the first star for balance, plus two twill lines on each side for selvage. This is abbreviated as: Dog Tracks = Star1 + Star2; woven piece requires // + 7(S1 + S2) + S1 + //. By counting the number of threads per harness in each motif and multiplying this by the number of repeats, I get a count of the number of threads per motif per harness, plus a total number of threads per harness, and a cross-check of the grand total of threads. The totals and how they are figured are labeled in the chart.

Before threading my loom, I move the correct number of heddles needed for each harness to the center of that harness. Then, while threading, I separate the correct number of heddles per harness for each motif and thread them. If I run short or have leftover heddles, I can immediately check the motif and not thread the entire piece before I realize a mistake has been made!

This chart is recorded on the back of my weaving record sheet, and below it I list treadlings and any notes or comments. On the front, I record information such as the date, pattern, threading, yarn, and sett. This chart can be made up prior to warping if the entire threading has been worked out precisely. If not—because you want to experiment, for example—it can be filled in after the fact.

Appendix B:
Finishing
Overshot Fabrics

All woven fabrics must be finished, but how they are finished is subject to great variation. Some of this variation is due to personal preference, and some to the type of materials and the function of the finished fabric.

I finish my coverlets (remember these are woolen coverlets) by first washing them as they come off the loom. This is a wash without soap; I use cold water and fabric softener in the gentle rinse and spin cycle of the washer. If the fabric is intended for use where a tighter finish is wanted, I switch to either the normal cycle, or warm water, or both. I hang the fabric on a wooden clothes dryer rack and gently shape it. When it is dry, any fringing, trimming, or sewing that is necessary is done. The last step is to steam iron the entire piece if needed (including the seams and fringes); this step depends on how soft or stiff the yarns are. In general, the softer yarns will not need the extra step of ironing.

Glossary

Accidental: Found in four-block opposites patterns, an accidental is a two-thread unit in the half-tone area. It is formed by the transition from one opposites block to another (e.g., 1,2,1,2,3,4,3,4).

Adjacency: In adjacent threadings and treadlings, successive blocks and harness combinations have elements in common with previous blocks and sheds. For example, a threading is 1,2,1,2,3,2,3 and its treadling 1-2,1-2,1-2,2-3,2-3,2-3.

As-drawn-in: Type of weaving; the shed sequence is identical to the threading sequence. If the warp is threaded 1,2,3,4, for example, the harnesses are treadled in the same order.

Balance: The relationship between the warp and weft yarns. If the warp and weft are of equal weight and show equally in the woven fabric, the weave is called *balanced*. If one or the other is dominant, the weave is *unbalanced*.

Block: Group of warp ends used together consistently in threading and treadling.

Broken twill: A point twill in which the threading progression from odd to even is interrupted by removing a warp end before or after the point; for example, 1,2,3,4,1,2,3,4,2,1,4,3,2,1.

Counterbalanced loom: A loom in which the shed opening is formed by the lowering of one or more harnesses. Also known as a sinking shed loom.

Draft diagram: A four-part notational system giving threading, tie-up, treadling, and pattern information (draw-down).

Draw-down: Representation of woven pattern on graph paper. The part of draft diagram that gives pattern information.

End: Individual warp thread.

Float: The part of a woven pattern that occurs when weft threads pass over two or more warp ends, or warp threads pass over two or more weft yarns.

Half-tone: Overshot pattern area, formed by common thread of adjacent blocks, consisting of one warp end.

Jack loom: A loom in which the shed opening is formed by raising one or more harnesses. Also known as rising shed loom.

Motif: In overshot, combination of blocks in specific formats to form units of pattern structure.

One-less rule: Number of shots of pattern weft per block in overshot weaving equals one less than the number of ends in the block.

Opposites: In overshot, opposites threadings and treadlings have successive blocks and harness combinations that do not have an element in common with previous blocks or sheds. For example, a threading is 1,2,1,2,3,4,3,4 and its treadling 1-2,1-2,1-2,3-4,3-4,3-4.

Overshot weave: Compound, twill derivative weave structure with tabby background and pattern of weft floats.

Plain weave: Weave structure with alternation of warp ends in forming sheds.

Point twill: A twill in which the threading changes directions instead of continuing in a straight progression; for example, 1,2,3,4,3,2,1 (point) in contrast to 1,2,3,-4,1,2,3,4 (straight).

Repeat: A pattern threading unit that is used a number of times to form the total threading draft; for example, a repeat of the Dog Tracks pattern (fig. 4-1) is two stars, one drafted on blocks A and B, the other on blocks C and D.

Selvage: Outside edges of the warp or woven fabric.

Sett: Number of warp ends per inch.

Shed: Warp opening through which weft passes. Formed by the action of harnesses rising (jack loom) or sinking (counterbalanced loom).

Shed sequence: Order in which harnesses or harness combinations are used to make sheds. Also called *treadling sequence.*

Shot: Passage of weft through shed opening.

Sley: The number of warp ends per inch. Also the number of warp ends drawn through each space, or dent, in the reed; e.g., *single sley* is one end per dent, *double sley* is two ends per dent.

Straight Progression: A sequence where the succession follows alphabetic or numeric order, such as 1,2,3,4 or A,B,C,D, rather than an unordered sequence such as 1,3,4,2.

Tabby: A balanced plain weave.

Threading draft: Representation of sequence in which ends are drawn in through the harnesses.

Treadling sequence. *See* Shed sequence.

Tie-up: Harness or harness combinations, connected to treadles, used for making sheds for weaving.

Twill weave: Weave structure characterized by diagonal pattern lines and overlapping shed sequence.

Undulating twill: A twill threading in which the threading progression from odd to even is interrupted by repeated warp ends in order to achieve undulating pattern lines; for example, 1,2,3,4,4,1,1,2,2,2,3,3,3,4,4,4,1,1,2,2,3,4.

Warp: Threads arranged lengthwise on loom.

Weft: Crosswise threads on loom, interwoven into warp to form woven fabric.

Bibliography

Anderson, Irma. "Ohio Coverlets." *Antiques*, January 1946.

Atwater, Mary Meigs. "The Coverlet as an Example of American Art." *House Beautiful*, vol. 56, no. 2 (1924).

———. "American Overshot Coverlets." *House Beautiful*, vol. 56, no. 3 (1924).

———. *Shuttle-Craft Book of American Handweaving*. New York: Macmillan Co., 1928.

Baily, Elizabeth C. *Man is a Weaver*. London: George R. Harrop & Co., Ltd., 1947.

Black, Mary E. *New Key to Weaving*. New York: Bruce Publishing, 1971.

Burnham, Harold, and Burnham, Dorothy. *Keep Me Warm One Night*. Toronto: University of Toronto Press, 1973.

Carstens, Annafreddie. "Handwoven American Coverlets." *Craft Horizons*, November 1948.

———. "Handweaving Coverlets Today." *Craft Horizons*, Spring, 1949.

Chase, William. *Five Generations of Loom Builders*. Hopedale, Mass.: Draper Corp., 1950.

Davison, Marguerite. *A Handweaver's Pattern Book*. Chester, Pa.: John Spencer Co., 1971.

———. *A Handweaver's Source Book*. Chester, Pa.: John Spencer Co., 1953.

Davison, Mildred, and Mayer-Thurman, Christa. *Coverlets: Handbook on the Collection of Woven Coverlets in the Art Institute of Chicago*. Chicago: Art Institute of Chicago, 1973.

Earle, Alice. *Home Life in Colonial Days*. New York: Macmillan Co., 1917.

———. *In Old Narragansett*. New York: Charles Scribner's Sons, 1898.

Eberlein, H. D., and McClure, A. *The Practical Book of Early American Arts and Crafts*. Philadelphia: J. B. Lippincott, 1916.

Estes, Josephine. *Miniature Patterns for Hand Weaving*. Part I (1956); Part II (1958).

Frey, Berta. *Designing and Drafting for Handweavers*. New York: Macmillan Co., 1975.

Gallinger, Osma. "Types of Overshot Patterns." *The Weaver*, vol. III, no. 2 (1942).

Hall, Eliza, C. *A Book of Hand-Woven Coverlets*. Boston: Little, Brown & Co., 1914.

Heisey, John. *A Checklist of American Coverlet Weavers*. Williamsburg, Va.: Colonial Williamsburg Foundation, 1978.

Huntley, Richmond. "The Woven Coverlet." *American Collector*, vol. X, no. 8 (1941).

Kurtz, Carol. "Designing Block Weaves." *Shuttle, Spindle & Dyepot*, vol. XI, no. 2 (1980).

Landes, John. *A Book of Patterns for Handweaving Designs*. Cambridge: Shuttlecraft Guild, Parts 1 and 2 (1925); Parts 3 and 4 (1926).

Lewis, Ethel. *The Romance of Textiles*. New York: Macmillan Co., 1953.

Little, Frances. *Early American Textiles*. New York: The Century Co., 1931.

Marston, Eva. "Ways to Weave Overshot." *Shuttle, Spindle & Dyepot*, vol. XI (1980).

Montgomery, P. *Indiana Coverlet Weavers and Their Coverlets*. Indianapolis: Hoosier Heritage Press, 1974.

Pariseau, George. "Weaver Rose of Rhode Island." *Handweaver & Craftsman*, vol. 6, no. 1 (1954).

Pocock, Sylvia. *A Basic Approach to Designing and Drafting Original Overshot Patterns*. North Myrtle Beach, S.C.: Sheriar Press, 1975.

Rabb, Kate. *Indiana Coverlets and Coverlet Weavers*. Indianapolis: Indiana Historical Society Publication, 1928.

Safford, C., and Bishop, R. *America's Quilts and Coverlets*. New York: E. P. Dutton, 1972.

Spruill, Julia Cherry. *Women's Life and Work in the Southern Colonies*. Chapel Hill: University of North Carolina Press, 1938.

Strickler, Carol. *A Portfolio of American Coverlets*. Loveland, Colo.: Interweave Press, no. 1 (1978), no. 2 (1979), no. 3 (1980), no. 4 (1981).

Swygert, Mrs. Luther, ed. *Heirlooms from Old Looms*. Chicago: R. R. Donnelley & Son Co., 1955.

Tidball, Harriet. *The Handloom Weaves*. Santa Ana: HTH Publishers, 1957.

———. *The Weaver's Book*. New York: Macmillan Co., 1976.

White, Margaret. *American Handwoven Coverlets in the Newark Museum*. Newark, N.J.: Newark Museum, 1947.

Windeknecht, Margaret. *Creative Overshot*. Shuttlecraft Guild, Monograph no. 1, 1978.

Windeknecht, M. and Windeknecht, T. *Color-and-Weave*. New York: Van Nostrand Reinhold Co., 1981.

Index